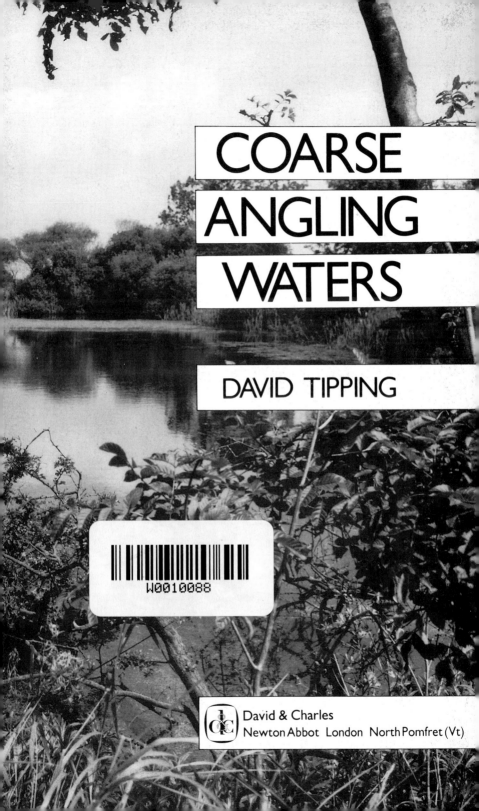

COARSE ANGLING WATERS

DAVID TIPPING

David & Charles
Newton Abbot London North Pomfret (Vt)

British Library Cataloguing in Publication Data

Tipping, David
  Coarse angling waters.
  1. Fishing—Great Britain
  I. Title
  799.1'1   SH605

  ISBN 0–7153–9165–8

Photoset in Linotron Ehrhardt by
Northern Phototypesetting Co, Bolton
and printed in Great Britain
by Redwood Burn Limited, Trowbridge, Wilts
for David & Charles Publishers plc
Brunel House Newton Abbot Devon

Published in the United States of America
by David & Charles Inc
North Pomfret Vermont 05053 USA

Contents

INTRODUCTION: *Coarse Fisheries*   7

1 BRIGGS PIT   11
A pool lavished with sunken trees: seeking jack pike as a
youngster, and progressing to large tench

2 THE RIVER WHARFE   33
Winter fishing for roach and chub on a day-ticket stretch of
the lower Wharfe

3 THE LAGOON   48
Big bream, rudd, carp and tench from an extensive gravel pit

4 THE RIVER NIDD   81
The difficulties of extracting barbel from a swim choked with
willow roots

5 CLAYDON LAKE   96
Hunting the outsize catfish of a famous Buckinghamshire
stillwater

6 SALLOW POOL   108
A very deep pond haunted by big perch, roach and eels

7 OAK BECK   127
Surprises from a small chalk stream in the shape of specimen
size pike and grayling

8 THE CROSS LANE PONDS   141
Seeking a handful of elusive carp on a shallow, weed-choked
pool

CONCLUSION   156

ACKNOWLEDGEMENTS   157

INDEX   158

Introduction:
Coarse Fisheries

Over the centuries, the face of our planet has been completely re-shaped by man, whose destructive influence has seldom taken into account the welfare of other life-forms. It is therefore strange to reflect that the spoils of an English landscape increasingly dominated by steel and concrete take the form of a multitude of pools, which have become havens for a diversity of wildlife.

There can be very few coarse fishing stillwaters which do not owe their creation to man, whether as a by-product of his need for raw materials or purpose-made to practical or ornamental specifications. The importance of these waters to the modern coarse angler is heightened by the decline in quality of many rivers as a result of abstraction, pollution and dredging.

In recent years, then, there has been a subtle shift of emphasis within coarse fishing as regards the waters on which the sport is practised. Most significant, perhaps, has been the emergence of gravel pits, born as a result of large-scale excavations to provide materials for the construction of our network of motorways. These immature waters are often very fertile, supporting luxuriant weed growth and a corresponding diversity of small aquatic animals, which provide rich pickings for the fish stocks. However, the clarity of most gravel pits betrays a shortage of the microscopic organisms which are essential to the survival of fry.

The result is that these extensive waters often harbour small populations of very large fish. Their nomadic habits contribute to an intriguing challenge for the angler, who must first consider the problem of location, and thereafter the difficulty of persuading fish to select a hook-bait from amid an abundance of natural food.

It would be a fair generalisation to say that small and middle-sized pools usually have a much longer history than gravel pits, and display considerable differences. Here we might be talking of old clay workings, perhaps dating back to times when men toiled with shovels and barrows. Flooded and long neglected, tree-hung

and rush-fringed, these places now bear no trace of the hustle and bustle of bygone years.

In these waters fry survival can be considerable, to the extent that fish become too numerous for the available food supply, resulting in a population of runts. Even in such situations though, there might be a handful of fish, perhaps of different species to the majority and dependent upon different food sources, which grow to a good size. Location is less of a problem here, for on small waters the quarry will always be close at hand. Old and wily inhabitants of such pools do not succumb easily to a bait, however, and will test any angler's ingenuity.

It has been said that river fishing demands more skill than fishing in pools, because of the difficulties posed by flowing water, but I do not subscribe to this view. While precise control of a float in a current can justifiably be described as a true art form, it is possible to reduce river fishing to something much less subtle and yet still achieve a degree of success. Angling is as skilful as the fisherman cares to make it, regardless of the type of water on which it is practised.

Rivers and streams, as habitats for fish, are less prone to extremes than stillwaters. Small fish from a flowing water are almost invariably immature as opposed to stunted, while the considerable energy expended by holding position in a current reduces the likelihood of fish growing to an exceptional size.

The richest running water environments occur in those streams which flow through chalk-based soils. Such waters usually support a lush growth of aquatic plants which, of course, form the basis of the food-chain upon which fish thrive and grow big. Many chalk streams are strictly preserved by game-fishing interests, but on those where there is access for the coarse angler, sport can be excellent. These are particularly productive winter fisheries due to the fact that they are usually spring-fed, and therefore not prone to flash floods and dramatic temperature fluctuations.

Rain-fed rivers, on the other hand, are subject to considerable change as a result of weather conditions. Fish respond to these changes in various ways, and for the angler the challenge lies in

A sizeable mirror carp

9

judging how they will react when one day a sharp frost might leave the river low and ice-cold, and the next it becomes a brown, swirling turmoil due to heavy rainfall.

Within the all-embracing term 'coarse fishing waters' come many other variations: estate lakes, the pride of nineteenth century aristocracy, beauty enhanced by years of neglect; canals, some derelict, some still plied by barges and pleasure craft; old quarry pools, sheer-sided and extraordinarily deep. Each water is unique, each poses new problems and a different challenge for the angler. All are fragile environments, at the mercy of nature's whims. Any might be destroyed overnight by man in a moment of carelessness.

The subsequent chapters are devoted to eight very different waters which between them contain all the species which the modern coarse angler is likely to encounter. The nature of each water has been examined, along with the wildlife which frequents the banks and of course the events leading up to and surrounding the capture of many fish. While the text does not delve more deeply than necessary into the technicalities of tackle, methods and baits, neither, I hope, is it flowery and romantic in style. Perhaps the reader will glean something of practical value from the following pages, but above all I hope he will taste the enchantment of angling for coarse species in a contrasting selection of fisheries.

1 Briggs Pit

My fishing at Briggs Pit began when I joined a local angling association, along with several school friends. Our attention was attracted to the water by one of the rules in the membership book, which requested that all pike caught from the fishery be removed. As schoolboys, we considered pike (even jacks) to be a very worthy quarry, and it wasn't long before a couple of my friends made the journey to the pit with a bucketful of livebaits. They came back bubbling with excitement after catching a 2-pounder, and hearing tales of much larger fish.

On hearing the news, I made arrangements to join them on their return visit. Firstly, however, the livebaits had to be replenished, but this was no problem because we knew of a small pond which seethed with tiny rudd. We spent many hours fishing the pond, believing as schoolboys do that swimming somewhere among those stunted fish was the grandfather of all rudd. We never caught it; in fact, I never saw a rudd from the pool which exceeded 4oz. It was the ideal place for catching large numbers of livebaits, however; and large numbers, according to my friends, were what we would need, for they told me that the pit was lavished with sunken trees in which many baits would be lost. In those days, of course, we had not heard of the float-paternoster, and our baits were allowed to roam freely, suspended a few feet below a small bung. It was always tempting to allow them to venture a little too close to the sunken trees, where we believed that pike would be waiting in ambush.

And so on a bitterly cold November morning, the three of us set off for the pit. The arrangement was that the father of one of my friends would drive us to the water, and my father would collect us at the day's end. It was still dark when I saw the headlights swing into the driveway; I picked up the tackle, ready and waiting, and opened the door to be greeted by the crisp, cold air. Soon we were rushing along country lanes in the grey half light, the bucket of livebaits slopping precariously at our feet. By the time we arrived it was full light; we stepped out onto frost-carpeted grasses and began unloading the tackle with feverish enthusiasm.

As the departing car rumbled away down the road, we were left in solitude before the glassy calm sheet of water. A more pikey looking place I would find hard to imagine. As pits go it was relatively small, covering an area of about 3 acres, and just as my friends had said, sunken trees were everywhere, ranging from small clusters of twigs protruding from the surface, to great tangles of branches which fingered up from the depths. Weed growth, even at this late stage of the year, was luxuriant. The predominant species was hornwort, which in places grew densely, forming a vivid, yellow-green carpet over the bottom. In one or two areas it reached to within inches of the surface. Rushes grew thickly in the margins, but they had lost the freshness of summer and were now tinted with yellows and browns. The water was pure and clear, and in the steeply shelving margins the bottom was plainly visible up to the point at which it melted into the shadow of the depths.

The banks were heavily overgrown with briars, nettle beds and a variety of grasses, but tree cover was sparse, restricted to a few willows and wind-warped hawthorns. In a corner near the entrance was a decaying brick building, presumably a relic from the days when the pit was operational. Close to this was an old, hand-painted blue caravan; this, I was to learn, was the home of an old Irishman who acted as the pit's bailiff. We came to know him as Paddy, and I can only describe him as the most likeable rogue I've ever met. He was no fisherman, but nevertheless had a host of fascinating tales to tell about the fish he had seen caught from the pit. Paddy had no steady job, making his living in any way he could, and we learnt with some amusement that he was banned from all three pubs in the local village. When I came of age I was often given the task of walking down the road to the nearest pub while Paddy guarded my tackle; his usual order was a quarter bottle of whiskey, sometimes with a bottle of Guinness thrown in for good measure. Evidently the landlord was familiar with this order, for on the very first evening that I walked into the pub, he guessed that I was a fisherman!

Back to the day in question; my two companions decided to share what they considered to be the best swim, but as there was not room for three to fish there, I was left to roam about the pool

alone. Several other anglers arrived to fish the pit, but there was
no action for anyone. We blamed the weather, which remained
bright and intensely cold. By mid-afternoon I had worked my way
round to the opposite end of the pit to that which my friends were
fishing. This area was well away from the main concentration of
sunken trees, but I found one swim, bordered by thick beds of
dry, yellow reeds, which looked distinctly pikey. There was a
solitary sunken tree to my left, a sprawl of gnarled branches which
clawed down into the darkness of the pool. It was here that I
expected pike to lie, if any were present. From a gap among the
reeds I lobbed my livebait close against the branches, but there
was no immediate response. After fifteen or twenty minutes, I
decided to wind in and set the float to fish the bait much deeper;
my friends had advised fishing at a depth of 2½–3 feet, in order to
facilitate keeping the baits out of the trees. As I was now fishing in
relatively clear water, however, this was no longer necessary.

Pretty soon the bung gave two violent bobs, and was then held
low in the water, before it eventually began to sink down into the
shadowy depths. My heart pounded strongly, as line trickled
through my fingers and slowly snaked away into the water. I gave
the fish plenty of time, and then drove the hook home. After a few
heavy pulls, a sleek little jack pike was hustled into the net with a
flurry of spray. I think my friends were a little jealous, even though
the fish weighed only ¾lb; not that it worried me, for I was well
pleased at having caught the only fish of any description taken
from the pool that day.

I enjoyed my first visit to Briggs Pit, and was eager to return. It
was the kind of wild, uncultivated place that I love to fish, and the
tales I heard about big pike hooked and lost among the sunken
branches added to the mystique. Unfortunately it was some
twenty miles distant from home, and as my friends and I had to
rely on our parents for transport, we were unable to fish it as often
as we would have liked. Every opportunity to visit the pit was
awaited with repressed excitement, for among the rushes and
sunken trees we always felt that a take from a pike was likely.
Oddly enough, we caught very little from the fishery apart from
pike. On occasions, when we found our livebait stocks running
low, we would attempt to replenish them by fishing a worm or a
maggot on light float tackle. More often than not, we failed to
tempt a bite. Paddy assured us that there were plenty of small

Portrait of a jack pike

perch and roach in the pit, but these were caught mainly during the summer. He also recounted fascinating tales about large tench – fish of 4, 5 or 6lb. In those days, however, tench were considered to be rather too sophisticated for our limited skills; the pike were always a more attractive proposition, although had we succeeded in catching the tench, I'm sure that our views would have changed.

My second visit to the pit was not until the following February. Having finally persuaded my father to take me, I secured a good supply of livebaits and awaited the big day with great excitement.

I was dropped off at about 9am on a mild, but dull morning without a breath of wind. I immediately headed for an overgrown corner of the pit, where there was a narrow channel of water bordered on both sides by thick beds of reeds. This was a swim which I had mentally noted on my previous visit as a likely pike spot. I rigged up my usual free-swimming livebait tackle, and

14

tested it out by lowering the rudd into the margins. The fish thrust away with great energy, while the bung wobbled erratically behind it. I lifted it out before it reached the reeds, and punched the tackle out to the end of the channel. There, the bung bobbed and jerked to the workings of the livebait, until after ten minutes the movements ceased; suddenly the float ran swiftly across the surface for a yard or so, until it came to rest again, brushing against the stalks of the reeds.

I was puzzled. The movements of the float seemed to be rather too deliberate to be caused by the bait, and yet not deliberate enough to be caused by a pike. But if the rudd had not been taken, it would now almost certainly be tangled among the reeds, so I decided that there was nothing to lose by striking. I did so; there was a heavy swirl among the stalks, and the rod lurched in my hands. Fortunately, the fish yielded to pressure, and then came begrudgingly down the channel. At close range it began to fight with more venom, repeatedly thrusting down towards the reeds. I could now see the pike in the clear water, a lean, dark form careering around within the confines which I imposed. Eventually it surfaced, jaws gaping, but it took several attempts to fit the fish into my undersized landing net. That pike taught me a lesson which I will never forget, for as I tried to unhook it, it clamped its jaws around my fingers. I was bleeding for some time, and at the end of the day had to visit the local hospital for a tetanus jab. There were a few raised eyebrows when I told the staff I had been bitten by a fish! The pike weighed 4¾lb, my biggest ever at the time of capture, and I spent a few moments admiring its mossy green form, flecked with primrose yellow, before slipping it back into the pit in defiance of the association rules.

Although our early efforts on the pool yielded only jacks, I remained convinced that it held some big pike; indeed, my friends claimed to have hooked and lost one or two, but the best which I witnessed would have weighed about 6lb. That one took a 4oz roach livebait offered by one of my friends, a much larger bait than we normally used. It was late afternoon, and for Alan the day had been uneventful; he had lost interest and started to mess about, when quite unexpectedly, his bung vanished. He played the fish out, but applied a little too much pressure as he drew it towards the net. The pike shook its head, and the tiny treble sprang free from its cavernous jaws.

15

I determined to try a large livebait on the next occasion that I fished the pit. It was on a warm August day that the chance arose. I took the livebaits from a local lake, where I managed to catch a number of fingerlings, plus the fish I wanted, a 4oz roach.

The big bait, and the large bung necessary to support it, made my flimsy rod seem totally inadequate, but with great effort I managed to heave the set-up a few yards out into the pit. The roach landed with a splash which left the water rocking; for a few moments it lay on its side, then suddenly there was an enormous swirl, and the bait was gone. The bung didn't move. I clutched the rod, heart pounding heavily, bale arm open so that line could be payed out if necessary. Still the bung didn't move; I took up a little line, and gently twitched it. This was the stimulus which the pike needed, and suddenly the float ran swiftly across the surface, a ripple in its wake, before coming to rest 10 yards further out in the pit. I wound down carefully, and then struck hard. The initial surge was of such power that for a while I thought I was into a lunker, but as the fight progressed it became clear that the fish was not as large as I had imagined. Soon it came wallowing towards the net, shovel-faced and evilly green; at 5½lb it was my biggest pike, but still a disappointment in some respects. Still the monster fish eluded me.

I fished the pit at irregular intervals for a number of years subsequent to that day, without catching, nor even hooking, a pike bigger than that 5½-pounder. I believed, and indeed still believe, that there were some sizeable fish which lay in the shadow of those sunken trees. I rarely fish the pit for pike these days; whether or not I will make another attempt to catch a big one, I don't know. I look back on my pike-fishing days at Briggs Pit with some nostalgia, and to return there and catch a 'double' would mean more than catching a bigger fish from elsewhere.

There is one particular day from that era which I must mention before I pass on to my more recent fishing on the pit. It was a November day, almost exactly a year since my first visit to the water, and the weather was bright and still. Four of us made the journey, with a good supply of fingerling roach livebaits. We found the pike in feeding mood, and took several jacks during the course of the morning. Shortly before lunch time there was some excited shouting, and I rushed along the bank to see what the fuss was about. A good perch had taken the livebait offered by one of

16

Early days on Briggs Pit. Pete Garwood and Tim Moulds pose with a catch of pike and perch

my friends. It weighed 1lb 3oz, and looked most impressive; in those days we regarded any perch of more than 4oz as large, and this was the biggest that any of us had ever seen. It seemed ironic that such a fish should fall to pike tackle after our efforts with worms and maggots had been so fruitless.

Later, I was fishing my favourite channel-in-the-reeds swim, when another friend announced that he was into a fish. He was fishing an impossible-looking swim situated behind an enormous hawthorn bush, and bordered by dense beds of rushes. There was hardly enough room to cast, and to make matters worse, there were a number of perilous-looking branches protruding from the water beyond the rushes. I heard a shout which sounded like 'It's terrific', and I immediately grabbed my landing net and rushed round to assist. I pushed beneath the hawthorn, and found my friend unhooking a perch of about 4oz, which had snaffled his livebait. Apparently he had shouted 'It's tiny', but in the excitement of the moment I had heard what I wanted to hear!

Clearly, a few perch were on the move that day, but at the time I thought nothing more of the capture of those two fish. By late afternoon our best livebaits had gone, and all that remained were

17

a few weaklings floundering at the top of the bucket. I killed one and lip-hooked it on a single size 6, tied direct to 8lb line; I was experimenting by fishing without a wire trace (not a good idea, I was later to discover).

I chose a swim where there was a large area of relatively clear water, bordered on the right by a line of sunken trees. I began to cast alongside the trees, allowing a minute or two for the bait to sink, and then wobbling it slowly and erratically back towards the bank. On the second or third cast, there was a pluck, then a heavy weight; I struck, unsure whether a fish was responsible or I had fouled weed on the bottom. Something began to yield slowly – a fish, but not a very lively one. It broke the surface with an oily swirl, giving me a glimpse of a spiked dorsal fin, and came to the net with just a few limp pulls in protest. Despite the weak fight it was a well-built and nicely conditioned perch, very dark, the stripes hardly discernible from the general colouration of the body. It weighed 1lb 1oz.

One summer, some years later, the association which owns the pit was negotiating the purchase of another, nearby stillwater, and members were allowed to fish there while negotiations took place. I made several visits during June, and discovered two particular swims which were far more productive for tench and crucians than the rest of the lake. The trouble was that everybody knew about these swims; other spots produced little apart from small rudd, ruffe and eels, so when I fished the lake I would aim to arrive well before dawn in order to procure one of the hot-spots.

One day I arrived late, and found the swims already occupied. I tried fishing elsewhere, but it seemed futile, so I caught a few small rudd and took them to Briggs Pit, intending to fish for pike. It was mid-morning when I arrived, and quite a few anglers were present. I noticed with interest that some of them were catching the small fish – mainly perch – which had eluded my friends and me when we attempted to supplement our livebait stocks. Most of our attempts at fishing worms and maggots had taken place in winter; it was clear that the small fish were much more easily caught on the pit during the warm months.

I managed to catch a few perch myself on that day. It was fascinating to watch the dark, stripy forms loom up from the shadow of the depths in response to loose maggots. More interesting, however, was the happening in a swim a little further down the bank from my own. I wandered round there to find an angler standing with a hopeless expression on his face, his rod hooped, but motionless. He told me that he'd hooked an unstoppable fish, which had snagged him solidly in the weed. My thoughts immediately flashed back to Paddy, and his tales of big tench. Also of interest was a catch being accumulated by an angler fishing among the reeds, directly across the pit from my swim. He was taking more perch than most, including one or two nice fish, and he also netted a modest tench of about 1½lb. I decided that the swim in which he was fishing was one to bear in mind for my next visit to the water.

One day in early July I headed for the new lake, arriving in darkness at 3am, but I found two anglers camping in the productive swims. Without wetting a line, I decided to head for Briggs Pit. In the grey half light, I pulled the car up against the old brick store-house, pleased to see that there were as yet no other anglers on the fishery. Gathering together my gear, I brushed through dew-soaked grasses, making for the swim among the reeds.

In the stillness of a summer dawn, the pit looked more attractive than ever. Mist drifted over the mirror-calm surface, which was broken occasionally by the dimples of small roach. Coots were already active among the protruding branches; the sound of their frequent squabbles carried through the still air with electrifying sharpness. To experience this twilight world while the rest of the human race sleeps is something of which I never tire.

I decided to commence by free-lining a lobworm, using an old-fashioned dough bobbin as a bite indicator. In those days I very much favoured resistance-free rigs, and avoided the use of lead or floats wherever possible – something which, in retrospect, I feel was a mistake. It wasn't long before a twitchy bite developed, and I landed a 6oz perch. Several smaller specimens followed, but not the hoped-for tench. As the sun began to climb, illuminating the reeded margins, I could make out a flotilla of tiny perch which were drifting slowly among the stalks. At some stage of the morning there was a sudden swirl, and a jack pike showed briefly among the milling fry. Having by now given up hope of catching a tench, I decided to offer one of my small perch as a livebait, but it brought no response.

At about this time, an old gentleman arrived to fish; we chatted briefly, and it transpired that I was fishing the swim which he rated as the best on the pool for tench. Then he wandered along the bank to try his luck elsewhere.

Not long afterwards I saw the door of Paddy's caravan open, on the other side of the pit. His dog hurtled out, soon to be followed by Paddy himself, standing in the doorway for a few moments and taking several deep breaths of fresh air. Shortly, he commenced his first round of the day, the familiar stooped figure, hands in pockets, ambling slowly along the bank and muttering the occasional Irish obscenity at the dog as it rushed round his feet. Some time later he arrived at my swim, still cursing the excited dog, and during our conversation he informed me that the old-timer had landed a tench of 4lb.

When Paddy departed, I took a stroll along the bank. I found the old man fishing from a gap among the marginal rushes, his attention focused on a red-tipped float which was positioned just a little beyond the rod end. After offering my congratulations on his catch, I asked if I might take a look at the fish, since at the time I had never seen a tench of such size. He invited me to lift out the keepnet, and there, nestling in the dripping meshes, I found a tench which to my eyes looked absolutely enormous. Breadflake was the bait, I was told, and a little mashed bread had been used to attract fish into the swim. He assured me that a similar fish was very much on the cards from my own swim, but urged me to make haste, since a hot day was in the offing and sport was likely to come to an end in mid-morning.

I returned to the swim and rigged up float tackle, as instructed, using a size 10 hook tied direct to 4lb line. Plumbing revealed a depth of about 8 feet just beyond the marginal rushes. I dropped in the bait, and followed up with a couple of handfuls of mash.

By now it was after 9am, and the sun was blazing down strongly; I felt that my chances of catching a tench were diminishing by the minute. About half-an-hour after casting out, however, and completely out of the blue, the yellow tip of my home-made goose-quill float gave a tiny dip and then slipped away. A sweeping strike made contact with a cumbersome, but powerful-feeling fish. It stayed deep, moving with short, heavy thrusts out into the pit, the reel handle revolving erratically as I grudgingly yielded line. After covering perhaps 10 yards the fish turned, and began to forge purposefully towards the bank of reeds to my right. Fortunately, however, it seemed reluctant to plunge among the slender stalks, preferring instead to struggle in open water. When it first broke the surface with an oily swirl, I saw that it was trailing a lost pike bung, attached to a length of line which had fouled my tackle during the fight. Before long, a big, spawn-filled female tench was drawn towards the net. It dwarfed any I had caught before, and registered 4¼lb on the scales.

There was to be no more tench action that day, but I was quite happy to while away my time in the warm sunshine, adding a few more small perch to my catch. I returned home at lunchtime, with thoughts only for the following morning, when I planned to have another crack at the big tench of Briggs Pit. Having discovered the method and the swim, I was confident of adding more fish to my tally.

Next morning, while it was still dark, I motored at speed along deserted roads and through sleeping villages. The headlamps sent bright shafts of light onto verges thickly tangled with the dense vegetation of high summer. Just once I glimpsed a pair of eyes glowing evilly in the distance – a prowling cat, or was it a fox?

The knotted mesh of the keepnet dates this picture of the author's first tench from Briggs Pit

I never found out, for it had melted into the undergrowth long before I reached the area.

By the time I had parked the car, the soft greys of early morning filled the sky. I rushed round to the swim and set up a float rig identical to that which I had used the previous day, except that I used 6lb line instead of 4lb. I wanted to be in a position to give those big tench some stick, if necessary. In no time at all my tackle was in position, with the bait resting over a carpet of mashed bread; the light was such that at this stage I still had to strain my eyes to see the float. There was no immediate response, however. Gradually the sky became brighter, and the early morning bats were replaced by the first swallows and martins of the day. A couple more cars pulled up, the occupants stepped out and the excited gabble of voices carried through the still air as they made for their swims. In the distance I heard the rattle of the first train of the day. Still my float remained unmoved.

It was now 7am; Paddy was up and out of his caravan, bright and early as usual. I was watching some tiny fry which were flipping in the reeds. Suddenly a small movement of the rod caught my eye; the float was nowhere to be seen, but the line remained limp. I waited for a second or two, then struck hopefully, but found myself fast into a snag. Eventually I had to pull for a break.

I re-tackled and re-cast, but another half hour of inactivity followed. Then, suddenly, the float twitched and vanished, but I unaccountably missed on the strike. I took comfort, however, in the fact that there now appeared to be a fish or two on the move.

Later still, I had just thrown in some more mash when the float gave a couple of tiny dips, keeled over and angled slowly away. This time there was no mistake, and I was into a fish which fought with vicious power and short, savage plunges. Making the most of my strong tackle, I hung on, with the rod bent into a wild hoop. Even so, it was a minute or two before the fish began to tire, giving me the first glimpse of a green flank as it rolled through the surface scum. It was a male tench, a dark-coloured fish with great black spades of fins. It weighed 3lb 9oz.

After staking out the keepnet I re-cast, expecting nothing more for a while following such a disturbance. But to my surprise the float was gone again within ten minutes, disappearing decisively following a preliminary twitch, a style of bite which seemed characteristic of the pit tench. The same violent struggle followed as the fish ploughed through the swim with deep, throbbing power; this time the fight was rather more prolonged. The tench eventually turned onto its side, and as I eased it towards the net I could see that it was another big, spawn-filled female. This one pulled the scales round to exactly 5lb; together the two fish made an impressive brace, the type of catch which just a few days previously seemed beyond my wildest dreams.

When Paddy passed by I told him of my success, and later in the day two doubtful anglers came round to ask if they could see the fish. Like myself, they had heard Paddy's tales about the pit's large tench, but they seemed to think that there was an element of exaggeration in his stories. When I pulled out my net they were flabbergasted, just as I had been the previous morning when I had seen the old man's 4-pounder.

Despite these results I didn't capitalise on the situation during the remainder of that summer. In fact I fished the pit on only one more occasion, this being a cool, breezy morning in mid-July. Once again I was at the water for first light, but I failed to tempt a definite bite. The only evidence of tench which I saw came when a dark back and a big spade of a dorsal fin cleaved the rippled surface, unfortunately well away from my swim.

I spent a great deal of time thinking about those tench during the following winter, and determined to spend more time on the pit come the new season. It was a pleasant place to fish, and I felt that a really big tench – possibly a 6-pounder – was on the cards. For some reason, however, I didn't fulfil my promise to myself, and during the next summer I again spent only a handful of sessions on the water. My first visit of the year proved to be an interesting one, however. Despite my limited experience with the tench, I had already formed certain conclusions about their behaviour; in particular, I believed that they always gave confident bites, and that it was a waste of time fishing for them after about 10am. It doesn't pay to be dogmatic about anything in fishing, as I was to discover.

It was early June, and I arrived at the pool shortly before first light, straining my eyes in the gloom to thread line through the rod-rings. I adjusted the shotting very carefully, so that just a fraction of an inch of the float's red tip poked through the surface, and in still very vague light conditions I cast out. The float sank, due, I thought, to the fact that I had cast into water deeper than the depth which I had set, causing the extra weight of the bait to submerge the tip. I drew the float a little closer to the bank, but again it sank. I drew it closer still; it lifted in the water, keeled over slightly, dithered a little and slid slowly away. A hard strike, and I was into my first tench of the season, savouring the short, powerful plunges until the fish eventually tired and broke the surface with an oily swirl. It was a stocky little male of 2½lb, which I slid into the keepnet prior to re-casting in anticipation of a good bag.

What followed, however, was a frustrating series of indefinite, dithering bites to almost every cast, and try as I might I couldn't hit them. Eventually one of these bites did develop, and I was into something good for a short while, but quite abruptly all movement ceased as the fish became solidly snagged. I tried everything to free it, but eventually I had to pull for a break. The association's efforts to clear some of the sunken trees have unfortunately left hidden tangles of roots on the pit's bottom; it is for this reason that I use strong tackle and bully-hooked fish, but inevitably some are lost from time to time.

So frequent were the finicky bites which I was getting that I thought roach, and not tench, were responsible. For this reason I opted to continue fishing with powerful tackle and a big hook and bait, hoping that sooner or later another tench would come along. By breakfast time, however, I still had only a solitary fish in the net, despite the fact that the shy bites continued so I decided on a change of tactics. I removed the size 10 hook and replaced it with a size 16, baiting with a tiny pinch of breadflake. I decided against using a light hooklength, trying the small hook direct to the 5½lb reel line; this left the tackle rather unbalanced, but the strong line was a valuable insurance against hooking a big tench among the roach which I expected. The original float was replaced with a tiny porcupine quill, fished top and bottom. I planned to hold the rod and strike at any positive indication.

First cast, the float dipped and I was into a lively fish which although not particularly large, gave a fight too prolonged and too powerful for a roach. A small tench of 1lb 2oz was eventually netted. This caused me to reconsider the cause of the finicky bites – perhaps a shoal of small tench was responsible? I re-cast, and was soon into another fish, but this one was clearly neither a roach nor a small tench. The fight was deep and heavy, and after a few minutes a big, green-flanked fish which I estimated at 4lb turned on the surface. This was to be my one and only glimpse of the tench, for shortly afterwards it dived and became immovably snagged among the sunken roots.

Having now suffered two losses to the roots, I decided that in the event of another good tench being hooked, I would hang on and not give an inch of line, risking having the hook straightened rather than allowing the fish to find sanctuary. Once again I flicked out the tackle, close against the marginal rushes, and followed up with a small ball of groundbait. Within minutes the float lifted and began to keel over; I struck as it did so and found myself into another big fish. I put my plan into operation and hung on. The tench went wild and the rod bent into a hoop, but the hook held and soon a solid 4-pounder was nestling in the meshes of the landing net.

With the morning now well advanced and the sun shining brightly, it came as something of a surprise that the tench were still willing to feed. There was time for one more, a 3½-pounder, before a light breeze began to ruffle the surface and bites dried up quite suddenly.

At one stage of the morning there was an interesting sidetrack which is perhaps worth recording. It came when a small jack pike of perhaps 5 inches long appeared among the reeds in the margins. These tiny pike can be contrary creatures, and I've often found them much more difficult to tempt than their larger brethren. When they show themselves in the margins, I always find it difficult to resist the temptation to offer them a bait, and so it was with this fish. To be honest I was expecting a negative response when I flicked a loose segment of worm in front of it. To my surprise, however, the pike followed the bait down, watched it for a few seconds as it lay on the bottom, and then scooped it up. I quickly pulled in my tackle, baited the hook with another segment of worm, and lowered it to the fish. The pike, along with a small perch, watched the worm as it wriggled on the bottom, and it was the pike which made the first move and picked it up, to be whisked ashore seconds later.

I've had some amusing sport with tiny jacks on hot summer days, when better fish cannot be persuaded to feed. The little pike can often be sought out as they bask amid weed, and will rarely refuse a freelined worm's tail, injected with air so that it floats. It's strictly fun fishing, of course, but it can be an enjoyable way to pass an hour or two.

It was through Paddy that I learnt that the association was planning to carry out some work on the pit, and what I heard worried me. I wrote a strong letter to the secretary, explaining my views on the matter, and I received an equally strong reply. Two years later Briggs Pit made the press, the association's work given coverage in the local paper and in both the angling weeklies. The banks were to be cleared and landscaped, in order to open up more swims, and more of the sunken trees were to be removed, to create what was proudly described as a 'parkland fishery'. Perhaps I'm selfish, but I liked the pit just the way it was; neither was I happy about the publicity which was suddenly thrust upon the fishery. I saw no reason to change my views following the completion of the work. The place looked a mess – flat, bulldozed banks, interspersed with saplings, tied to stakes, which were planted willy-nilly around the pool, often directly behind good swims where they would grow to hinder casting. Sunken trees had been dragged out here and there, leaving more hidden roots in hazardous positions. And to cap it all, as a result of the publicity, the once neglected fishery was suddenly subjected to a quite substantial increase in angling pressure.

It is true that when the seeded banks developed a covering of grass, the place regained a little of its former attraction, but for me it has never since had quite the same appeal. In the year following the work I finally did what I had promised to do for so long, and devoted considerably more time to fishing the pit. This came about because I had acquired a job not far from the fishery, and it was a convenient place to travel for after-work sessions on summer evenings. Indeed, I fished the pit almost every day during the first month of the season. I felt sure that a concentrated effort would eventually produce a real brute of a tench. This was not to be, although I believe that I came close to catching such a fish on one occasion, more of which later.

I caught tench on most of my visits to the pit, my first fish of the season being the biggest at 4¾lb. It seemed that the tench population was undergoing changes, which were noticeable even in the space of the few seasons that I had been fishing for them.

Briggs Pit today. Many of the sunken trees have been removed

The fish seemed to be becoming more numerous, with a greater preponderance of small samples in the 1–2lb range featuring in catches. Whereas at one time three or four bites in a session was the norm, now it was not unusual to get a dozen or more. The bites were much sharper and more difficult to hit, however, which I attributed to the fact that the fish were becoming shy as a result of increased angling pressure. Indeed, many of the tench began to show signs of having been caught before, in the form of distorted mouths and tatty fins. All in all, it seemed that the tench fishing on the pit was past its peak, and that the chance of an outsize fish was diminishing rapidly.

I had some interesting sport with roach during this period. It started when I spoke to a couple of anglers who were sharing a swim; they had good roach boiling for loose-fed casters, and reckoned to have several fish which averaged 2lb apiece in their keepnet. I saw those roach when the two anglers packed up. The largest probably weighed about 1¼lb, but they were nevertheless

27

a nice stamp of fish, and the next day I travelled to the pit armed with a pint of casters.

I soon had roach on the go; it was only necessary to drop in a dozen casters beneath the rod tip, and dark shapes would materialise from nowhere, flanks flashing silver as they mopped up the feed. Catching them was another matter, for despite the fact that I scaled down to a 22 hook and a 1lb bottom, they were well aware of the difference between the hookbait and the loose feed. I had bites alright, but they were lightning fast and near impossible to hit because the bait was ejected within an instant of being taken. I managed to take some nice fish, all in the ½–1lb range, by fishing with just a foot of line between the rod tip and the float, and tightening gently at the first suggestion of a bite. I still missed many takes for each one which I hooked, however. It was hard work, but nonetheless thoroughly enjoyable fishing, made worthwhile by the sight of those deep-flanked, bronze-tinged fish. The shoal remained in the area for several days, and then disappeared quite suddenly. Never before or since have I seen good roach in such numbers on the pit.

Meanwhile, I had almost given up hope of taking an outsize tench. One evening, however, I struck at a bite on the usual floatfished breadflake, and found myself into an immensely powerful fish. It moved slowly and deliberately towards the sunken trees on the right hand side of my swim, and in a desperate effort to keep it out I applied all the pressure I could muster with my 5½lb line. There was a piercing crack, and the fish was lost. Friends have since suggested that it might have been a carp, or an ordinary sized tench which was foulhooked. Well, the fish fought in characteristic tench fashion, so I think I can discount the possibility of a carp. I concede that the fish might have been foulhooked, but I doubt it. Paddy claimed to have seen tench up to 7lb caught from the pit, and I have a strong feeling that I was briefly connected to one of those big, old fish.

One evening, Paddy sent me to the pub for a slightly different order than usual. He wanted a half bottle of whiskey, and two bottles of Guinness. I duly returned with the drinks, upon which he disappeared into the caravan, emerging a few minutes later with two dirty mugs, each half-filled with whiskey. He handed

A sleek female tench of 5lb 7oz

one to me; apparently it was his 72nd birthday. We sat on the banks of the pit drinking and talking, until Paddy eventually retired to the caravan to drink himself into oblivion. Fishing on the pit was never dull when Paddy was around. His character is impossible to portray in words, but I never met an angler (apart from the odd poacher) who disliked him. One amusing incident which always stands out in my memory occurred on a July morning, when a friend and I had made a dawn start and put a few tench into the net. Come mid-morning, with the tench sport finished, I decided to fish a small plug for the remaining hour or so before we packed up to take a pub lunch. It wasn't long before it was snapped up by a jack of about 1½lb. Paddy watched as I unhooked the fish; he was evidently under the impression that I was still fishing for tench, for he came up with the observation 'Jaysus, the beggar has teeth like a pike!'

Oddly enough, I have fished the pit on only a handful of occasions since that month of intensive fishing. The reasons for this are several. As I said, I felt that the fishery lost some of its magic when it was landscaped, and when the number of anglers began to increase. Also, it seemed that the chance of a really big tench was much slimmer than I had at one time suspected. But more than anything, I think that I fished the pit too often in a short space of time, and simply burnt out my interest in it. It was like a love affair which had grown, become too intense and then crumbled.

I only ever caught four different species from Briggs Pit – pike, perch, tench and roach – but Paddy assured me that other species were present. I didn't catch the big eels, largely because I never fished methods which were likely to catch them. The pit supposedly contained a few bream and some chub, but I never saw them. I was most interested when Paddy told me that some big rudd were present; I wondered if perhaps they were the unused livebaits which my friends and I had released in some numbers during our pike-fishing days.

Nowadays my occasional visits to the pit are made mainly for the nostalgia which the place holds for me. I fished there on a bleak February day not so long ago, hoping, as I had hoped so often before, that I might contact one of those elusive big pike. Snow had fallen during the previous night, and had drifted in the strong winds so that it was several feet deep in some places, while

the bank was exposed in others. I chose a swim in which I could fish with the wind behind me, and erected an umbrella to afford some shelter. Conditions were appalling, and I knew that any fish would be a bonus on such a day.

I set up a freeline rig and mounted a sprat on the snap tackle, casting out alongside a row of sunken trees before settling in the lee of the wildly flapping umbrella. Nearby a solitary mute swan uttered an occasional hoarse croak as it drifted close to the leaning reeds, and one or two coots were bobbing among the waves. A wisp of smoke emerged from the chimney of the caravan, and later in the day I saw Paddy emerge, well wrapped up, with dog and shopping bag, heading for the village.

I picked up the rod and gave two or three sharp twitches to the line, in order to impart life into the sprat, and after a pause of a minute or two, the procedure was repeated. During the second pause, the line between the rod tip and the water gave a distinct twitch, and simultaneously I felt a tug. I waited for a moment; nothing further happened so I wound-down and struck. The heavy weight which I encountered appeared at first to be caused by a substantial fish, but it began to yield and when it eventually rolled, leaving a calm patch in the wind-rippled surface, I knew that it was just another jack. It weighed 4½lb, a fish which evoked memories of better times on the pit. I've often wondered how I would have fared, had I been able to fish for the tench in those early days with the ability and the technique which I now possess. I can't help feeling that I was ten years too late for the best of the tench fishing on Briggs Pit.

On a recent visit to the fishery I learnt that Paddy had died. The pit will never be the same again.

2 The River Wharfe

While the lower Wharfe has a justified reputation for producing quality roach, fishing for them is a chancy business; they're fickle fish, very much influenced by conditions, and rather localised in their distribution along the river. During summer, river roach tend to be very nomadic, difficult to pin down and not easy to tempt with baits due to the abundance of natural food which is available. In winter, however, the fish roam less and often congregate in certain, favoured areas where, given suitable conditions, the angler may seek them with a reasonable chance of success.

The most favourable winter conditions occur following heavy rain, which swells the river with floodwater. Those who practise their fishing on more placid waters would be surprised by the way a Yorkshire spate river can change following rain, to become a turmoil of brown, swirling water which moves with majestic force. Weirs become mere furls on the surface, and more than once I've seen the Wharfe burst its banks and flood the surrounding fields, until the course of the river was lost in a vast lake. At such times it is not unknown for water to be lapping at the doors of riverside houses.

Spate rivers are dangerous places in high floods, and over the years there have been a few tragedies, of which the Wharfe has seen its share. However, a much lesser watercourse will perhaps better illustrate my point. The Crimple Beck, a tributary of the River Nidd, is a shallow, rocky trout stream, an innocuous place in normal conditions, but very different following heavy rains. There was an autumn day, more than a decade ago as I write, when the beck was running high and turbulent, swollen by floodwater. A young lad apparently lost his footing while climbing an overhanging tree; his body was found by a farmer the following day, face down in a flood pool, over a mile downstream.

Conditions of extreme high water are not conducive to the best in roach fishing, but in a lesser flood they can be sought in deep, bankside slacks where they gather, along with various other species, to escape the force of the main current. Sport can be brisk at such times, and there is added interest because you can never be sure what will take your bait next; chub, dace and of course roach are the most likely catch, grayling and perch are always on the cards and there is a chance of something less usual, such as an unseasonal bream or barbel. The height of a flood can be productive, but perhaps the best period of all comes when the river has fined down, but still carries a touch of colour and runs a little above normal level. Rising water is generally less favourable, although I recall a wild January day of gusting wind and rain when the level rose by 3 feet in the course of an afternoon, forcing me to move up the bank on several occasions; despite this, some nice roach fell to stret-pegged maggots.

There are, I think, three fundamental reasons for the fact that flood conditions are so productive for the winter roach angler. Firstly, a flood generally causes a slight increase in water temperature (it should be noted that the reverse is true in summer, and that this might not apply where snow broth is concerned). Secondly, light penetration is impeded by colouration of the water, and roach are accepted to feed best in low light levels. And thirdly, during floods large numbers of roach may congregate in small areas in order to escape heavy currents.

In certain circumstances, however, my experiences suggest that flood conditions are not favourable; I refer to the deep, slow-flowing stretches of river which usually precede weirs. Roach gather in numbers in such places during the autumn and remain there throughout the winter. These stretches are often fairly uniform in depth and width, and consequently there is an absence of slacks of the type in which roach might congregate during a flood. Odd fish might be tempted by fishing tight in the margins, but generally I have found normal river levels to be preferable.

One of these deep, slow-flowing stretches, which spans a distance of about a quarter of a mile above a weir, is situated on the outskirts of a small market town. I first fished this part of the Wharfe as a child, and since then there have been many changes. In those days the river was quite remote, the town set some distance away, and the banks shared only by other anglers. Since then the town has gradually expanded, until now only the crack willows and sycamores on the far side separate the river from the

Winter scene on the River Wharfe

nearest houses. Increasingly the bankside path has become used by dog walkers and those out simply for a stroll. Yet despite all this intrusion, the river has always retained something of the magic it held for me during childhood.

This is heavily fished day-ticket water, capable of producing big fish of several species. As on any part of the Wharfe, or indeed any Yorkshire river, sport fluctuates considerably in relation to conditions; nowhere have I found this to be quite so noticeable as on this stretch, however. There are days, all too rare, when fish come to almost every cast – dace in abundance, gudgeon, grayling, perch, small roach and from time to time something bigger, usually a chub. There are other days, rather more common, when despite apparently good conditions, it is a struggle just to tempt a bite.

It is common knowledge that decent roach inhabit this part of the river, but few anglers fish selectively for them. Small ones are caught in fair numbers by fishing maggots on fine tackle, and from time to time anglers using such tactics find themselves attached to a better specimen. It happened to me on one occasion when I struck at a tiny, dipping bite while stret-pegging, and hooked a fish which gave a dour, deep struggle before yielding to the net – 1lb 1oz. Then there was the angler who grassed a monster while in the process of accumulating a double figure net of dace; that one weighed a fully authentic 3lb 5oz, and is generally accepted to be the largest river roach ever landed in Yorkshire.

It was, I suppose, a catch of perch which indirectly resulted in my getting to grips with some of those big Wharfe roach. As a child I quite frequently witnessed nice perch taken from the stretch, fish of around a pound in weight. It became a burning ambition to catch one, so much more impressive were they than the stunted pond perch to which I was accustomed, but I failed due to the fact that my skills were so limited. Then came a time when the perch were no more; the disease which decimated stocks throughout the country finally reached Yorkshire. For several seasons perch were unknown on the Wharfe, but in the early 1980s odd ones, mostly small samples in the 4oz to 8oz range, began to crop up among catches again.

On a bright early November day I travelled to the river, electing to fish a favourite swim marked by a bare, sandy area of bank among the wilted remnants of the summer vegetation. In the margins the depth drops steeply into a depression in the river bed, which although only slightly deeper than the surrounding area has proved to be a feature which attracts fish. On the day in question the river was running a few inches higher than usual, following recent rain, and was carrying just a tinge of colour. There was an intermittent, light upstream breeze, which fortunately wasn't strong enough to hinder my fishing.

There is nothing I enjoy more in such circumstances than to watch a stick float, shotted until the merest dot of yellow hangs in the surface film, drifting gently with the current, and to feel the thump of a hooked fish through the delicate curve of a carbon match rod. For bait I had brought along a pint of casters, which I planned to fish on a barbless number 24 hook and a light hook-length of 1lb breaking strain nylon. A centrepin reel completed the outfit. The depth I knew to be around 9 feet, and I set the float accordingly.

Autumn was well advanced, the branches of the far bank trees having lost the bulk of their russet-coloured leafage, although fortunately the dead leaves which can be such a menace as they drift down-river at this time of year were not evident in large numbers. Flicking the tackle into the flow, I followed up with a few loose casters and watched the float move slowly through the surface reflections. Bites began to come at once, but the culprits were invariably small fish, mostly roach of a few inches long with a handful of slightly larger dace thrown in. I fished on, however, peppering the surface with casters before each cast, aware that better fish might move into the swim in response to the loose feed at any moment.

I'd been fishing for perhaps a little short of an hour when, following one of the few occasions when the float ran through without signalling a bite, I decided to hold back at the end of the trot so that the bait lifted enticingly off the bottom. The half-cocked float drifted across the flow before settling directly down-stream of the rod tip, where it occasionally weaved sideways a little in the current. Suddenly it submerged, unhurriedly but quite deliberately, and upon tightening I realised at once that I had a decent fish. It made a short, but heavy run out into the river, the centrepin revolving under light finger pressure, and then it hung deep, thrusting forcefully in the current. I suspected a chub, but as the fight progressed and the fish continued to struggle doggedly within a confined area, an uneasy feeling developed that it might be nothing more than an unseasonal eel. Gradually I began to coax it upwards, until before long I glimpsed a fleeting, pale gleam as it turned in the murky water, but this initial sighting was not enough to enable me to identify the fish. Suddenly a sizeable perch broke the surface, flank glistening momentarily in the weak autumn sunshine before it plunged once more. A flurry and a swirl in the ripple, and it was hustled over the rim of the outstretched net.

It was a perch larger than any I had previously seen taken from this part of the river, even in pre-disease days, though I don't doubt that fish of such size have always been present. After recording a weight of 1¾lb I resumed fishing and took several more perch during the next hour, all of good size although none equalled the first one. Then, as suddenly as they had arrived, they were gone again, and thereafter my efforts yielded only more

37

small roach and dace. The catch reflects a general improvement in perch fishing on the Wharfe in recent years, although my attempts to contact those fish again have so far proved fruitless.

The following day saw a marked deterioration in the weather, skies of sombre grey and long periods of rain. On this occasion I had available a container of lobworms, but I elected to begin by fishing casters beneath a stick float again. Plenty of small roach and dace fell to this tactic, but nothing better. In mid-afternoon I decided to retreat beneath the umbrella to shelter from the rain, which had become rather heavy, and to change to a quivertip outfit and a lob-tail bait with the aim of tempting perch. Two swan shots were enough to hold bottom in the gentle current, and after tightening so that there was a slight curve in the quiver, I sat down to await events.

There was just a solitary, missed bite until 4pm, by which time it had become very gloomy as the November night drew in. It was then that the quiver gave several sharp jags; I lifted the rod and felt contact made with a fish which in truth gave a rather feeble struggle, swimming meekly into the margins where it gave a few half-hearted plunges and a heavy swirl or two before yielding to the net. It was a roach, a thick-set, deep-flanked fish of 1lb 2oz which looked strong and healthy despite the poor fight.

A little later I hooked something which was altogether more lively, plunging determinedly in the current until the hook pulled free. I strongly suspected another roach, and judging by the struggle, rather larger than the one I had just landed. Despite the rain and a rather awkward downstream wind which had sprung up, I decided to fish into darkness; I found the quiver quite easy to see in the light from the far bank houses. There were several more sharp bites, but I succeeded in landing only a large tommy ruffe and a bootlace eel.

Two further sessions spent fishing lob-tails produced several species of fish, including another nice roach of 1lb 5oz. Both times I fished into darkness, hoping to capitalise on the fact that big roach are very much nocturnal in habit, but both times my efforts were frustrated by unseasonal eels. It had been a very mild autumn, and even though it was now mid-November, there had as yet been no severe frosts, which perhaps accounts for the fact that eels were still in evidence. In retrospect, the obvious solution to the problem would have been to fish with bread baits rather than worms. It was with bread that Tony Smith approached the fishing on several occasions that autumn; most of his actions came from chub, but he managed to land one very fine roach of 1lb 11oz. He found, as I had done, that bites were very much concentrated into the first hour of darkness.

My next visit to the river took place in mid-January, following a spell of bitterly cold weather which put paid to any chance of being pestered by eels; nevertheless I elected to fish with bread as bait. On the day in question there were traces of snow on the ground, following a light fall some days earlier, and the river was running low and clear. The air temperature was a little warmer than it had been of late, but nevertheless conditions were a long way from ideal for roach fishing. It should be said that in some of these deep stretches which precede weirs, roach sport can be brisk during very cold weather, but on the length in question I have rarely achieved good results in such conditions.

After mashing a few slices of bread in water so cold that my fingers turned numb, I introduced it to the swim in small balls so as to create a bare minimum of disturbance. A running Arlesey bomb served to anchor the bait, which was a small cube of crust on a number 14 hook, attached to a short hooklength of about 4 inches of 2-pound breaking strain line. This set-up was geared to some degree towards chub, which I felt to be the most likely catch on the day in question, and for which I have found a short hooklength to be very successful during the winter months. I'm not sure why this is so; perhaps the short hooklength acts like a bolt rig, turning finicky bites into strong pulls. Whatever the reason, I have proved to my own satisfaction that in many winter chubbing situations, short hooklengths equate with more hooked fish.

Conditions were such that the fishing was always destined to be a struggle, and it came as no surprise that the quiver remained motionless for the first hour. A switch to maggot, fished beneath a stick float, brought no response either; as a last resort I headed up-river, to the streamy water above the deeps, where I hoped to find a few grayling in feeding mood, but even they wouldn't oblige. In late afternoon, as the light began to fade, I returned to the sandbank and lobbed out a little more mash, which brought the resident, semi-tame mallards winging swiftly towards the area in misguided anticipation of a feed. Several birds splashed down, loud quackings filling the still evening air, but the bread had long since gone, clouding and flaking down through the current. I baited with a portion of crust and cast out, tightening to the bomb until the quiver was under slight tension. The ducks gradually drifted away, and I settled on the chair to wait. Before long the quiver gave a sharp jab; it had sprung back long before I had a chance to strike, but suddenly my interest was renewed. Two more of these fast, nervous indications followed, and I geared myself for an immediate strike in response to the next movement of the tip.

By now the light had all but gone; a blackbird called sharply and repeatedly from somewhere among the far bank trees prior to settling to roost, clearly audible above the distant drone of the town traffic. Church bells chimed, and a glance at my watch confirmed the time at half past four. Suddenly the quiver, now just a thin white line visible against the dark reflections on the river's surface, gave a gentle nudge, and I hovered over the rod handle in anticipation. Seconds passed, until it seemed that nothing further would happen; then the tip stirred, and without pausing for thought I swept the rod sideways. The carbon hooped tightly against something which hung deep and unmoving in the placid current. Slowly, almost imperceptibly, it began to cut up the flow; I tried to follow its movements by watching the curve of the rod, silhouetted against the dusk sky. Suddenly the struggle became more urgent, several short, forceful thrusts causing the tip to jag downwards, and then it slowly dawned on me that the resistance against which I was straining the tackle had become unmoving; the fish had run into a snag on the river bed. Nagging doubts about the wisdom of using light tackle were quickly dispelled though, when an increase in pressure was answered by a heavy pull, and I was in business again.

Gradually the fish weakened, its movements becoming more restricted, until it broke the surface in an oily swirl. Several more determined plunges were thwarted before it surfaced again, beaten now; in the gloaming I was able to distinguish a sizeable chub, mouth agape as it wallowed over the rim of the net. After slipping the hook from its lips I admired it for a moment – the thick back, the neat, sharp outline of the scales, orange-tinted fins and the dark, almost black spread of the tail. It weighed 4¼lb, and but for a rather hollow belly it might have been heavier. Lifting the chub from the wet meshes, I felt the icy coldness of its flanks before slipping it back into the margins.

Three more good bites were missed, each pulling the quiver round strongly, before the feeding spell came to an end. The introduction of more mash failed to bring a further response, so I tackled down in the light of the far bank houses, well pleased to have grassed a good fish in far from favourable conditions.

A week later I returned in conditions which were, if anything, even less favourable. Snow had fallen, a thick mantle of white covering the ground, contrasting sharply with the inky darkness of the river, which was still running low and clear. It was one of those sombre, damp winter days when droplets of moisture accumulate on branches and twigs, and consequently the margins close to the far bank were constantly dimpled by the dripping trees. I made no attempt to arrive early, knowing that action was unlikely before dusk. It was lunchtime when I walked the riverside path, adding to the many footprints and paw prints before depositing my tackle on the unmarked crust of snow at the water's edge.

Tactics were the same as the previous week, except that I chose to bait with flake rather than crust. After feeding the swim with a little mash I sat back to wait, expecting and indeed getting no bites during the course of the afternoon. The mallards were in evidence again and I decided to spare them a little bread, which I threw in some twenty yards down-river rather than have the birds squabbling in the swim. This offering was gratefully accepted, every crumb polished off quickly as the ducks and a handful of gulls competed noisily. Another less prominent bird, a pied wagtail, kept flitting across the river to alight nearby, upon the skeletal stalks which protruded above the snow. Since it too appeared to be hungry, I used my wellington boots to make a clearing in the snow at the water's edge, and scattered some maggots on the exposed sand. A short while later I saw that the wagtail had discovered the maggots and was picking them up one by one, giving them a good shake, manipulating them in its beak and swallowing them.

In late afternoon I introduced a little more mash to the swim and from then on, events followed a very similar pattern to those of the previous week. In the fading light at 4pm came the first, shy movement of the quiver, and half an hour later, in near darkness,

41

came the first of two fish hooked in rapid succession, chub of 3lb 7oz and 3lb 5oz; both gave slow, heavy struggles in the icy river as I watched the now familiar arch of the carbon against the dusk sky, in an effort to keep track of their movements. More missed bites followed, but after perhaps an hour of darkness action diminished and I decided to replenish the mash. This had the effect of killing the swim completely.

Several further visits to the river during the final weeks of the coarse season failed to produce any more fish. Each of these visits coincided with periods when the river was carrying a little extra water; bites to bread came during the middle of the day, tailing off towards dusk, and were invariably very delicate, despite the fact that I experimented with different terminal rigs in an attempt to induce confident takes. I suspect that these bites came from small fish – dace and roach – which often show in considerable numbers at times when the river carries a touch of extra water and colour. As previously stated, in deeps above weirs I believe low water to be preferable for quality roach, and I'm inclined to think that this applies to chub, too.

Summer fishing on this part of the Wharfe tends to be poor, so it wasn't until mid-October that I returned to the river. The sandbank swim was occupied when I arrived, so I elected to fish from a position about 30 yards downstream, where I knew the depth to be rather less. However, careful plumbing revealed a sharp drop-off, about a third of the way across the river, beyond which the water was reasonably deep; I decided to concentrate my attack on this area.

The autumn had been a mild one, with no severe frosts so far. The sycamores and crack willows on the far side still carried the bulk of their leafage, although the freshness of summer had gone and they were now tinged with yellow. There were still traces of Canadian pondweed in parts of the margin, the presence of which reflects the gentle, almost non-existent flow in this part of the river during normal summer conditions. Mild weather, lingering vegetation; would fish have moved to their winter haunts, or would the deeps be devoid of all but the summer residents such as eels and ruffe?

I decided to start by fishing a single white maggot on gossamer tackle, pulling large loops of line from the centrepin so that I was able to flick the small, wire-stemmed stick float out to the drop-off. Fine, dry weather over a period of several weeks had left the river running so low that the current was negligible, and the yellow-tipped float crept downstream so slowly that its movement was almost imperceptible.

An uneventful day followed; I concluded that, as feared, fish had still not moved into the deeps in numbers, but nevertheless as dusk approached I found myself tempted to rig up a quivertip outfit in the hope that an odd roach or chub might show with the onset of darkness. Bait, as usual, was flake, fished on a number 14 hook which was tied to a long hooklength (2½ feet) of 2lb nylon. Rather than introduce mash by hand, I decided to pack it into a small, open-end feeder, which was attached to a fixed link of about 9 inches long. In this way, small amounts of mash would be introduced to the swim on a regular basis which, I hoped, might persuade fish to linger in the area for a little longer than was usually the case when a solitary, large baiting was made before the expected feeding period. Also, the feeder ensured that mash reached the bottom in a compact area, close to the hookbait. In theory, the use of a feeder seemed like a good idea, but in practice, on this and other stretches of river, results were little different to those achieved by straight legering. In fact, since then I have for certain reasons reverted to ordinary legering for most of my bread fishing on rivers.

Back to the day in question. At dusk, the light breeze which had been evident dropped to nothing. There was a distinct autumnal nip in the air, but not enough to deter a bat which was flitting high above the river, clicking wings clearly audible in the stillness. Soon now it would respond to the falling temperatures by seeking out some dark, sheltered place to hibernate, passing the hard months dormant until aroused again by the warm days of spring.

Meanwhile, two tiny movements of the quiver which came soon after casting out the feeder rig were encouraging, but thereafter there was nothing until 6.30pm, by which time the light had almost gone. It was then that there came a gentle nudge of the tip, following which it pulled round a little before springing back; sitting bolt upright in the chair, I waited, hand poised over the rod handle. The pause was a long one, but I was ready for the slow pull of the quiver when it came; the strike made contact, and immediately I had to yield line to the heavy rush of the freshly hooked fish. After taking a few turns from the reel it slowed and hung deep in mid-river, thereafter yielding grudgingly. Beneath the rod tip it suddenly came to life again, forging powerfully to the left and diving among the overhanging grasses which trailed in the water. There were several heavy swirls and crashes before the chub was drawn back into the open river, and soon to the net.

In many respects it resembled the 4¼-pounder which I had taken at the beginning of the year; a touch of bronze on the flanks, generally in good shape but perhaps a little hollow in the belly. When the scales settled at 4lb 3oz, I wondered if in fact it was the same fish. I'll never know for sure, since the chub taken in January was returned without being photographed.

The first severe frosts of that winter came with a vengeance in early November, and for long periods of the month the weather remained bitterly cold. A slight rise in temperature during the third week tempted me to venture to the river again, confident now that fish would be present in the deeps in reasonable numbers. The chosen day was not a pleasant one, being grey and still quite cold, with a light, but biting downstream breeze. There was also a little fine rain which came in frequent spells of brief duration, hardly warranting the erection of an umbrella, but disagreeable just the same.

The day was spent fishing maggots beneath a stick float. Tackle control proved to be difficult in the low, clear river, since the breeze tended to push the float through the swim a little faster than the speed of the current. In retrospect, a change to a different float might have solved the problem. I struggled to catch half a dozen small roach and dace, all much of a muchness at a couple of ounces apiece. In late afternoon, as the light began to fade, I dismantled the float tackle and picked up the quivertip rod. The terminal set-up consisted of the usual fixed link, 2lb hook-length and number 14 hook; two swan shots would, I knew, be more than enough to hold bottom in the gentle current. The mash was introduced just a little upstream of the intended fishing area, taking into account the effect of the flow, and then a pinch of flake was squeezed onto the hook. The current was so weak that I was able to tighten to the shots and leave the quiver under minimal tension, just very slightly curved.

More fine rain drifted down on the cold breeze. Now that I was engaged in a less active form of fishing, I felt it worthwhile to set up the umbrella, which afforded protection from the worst of the

Quality roach and chub taken from the Wharfe on a January evening

weather. It wasn't long after settling beneath it that the quiver started nodding; my first reaction was to wait for a strong pull, but it quickly became apparent that something had confidently accepted the bait, so I struck. The rod clattered against the rim of the umbrella, but nevertheless a fish was hooked; while it felt to be of reasonable size, it lacked the power of a chub, and that left only one other likely possibility. My hopes were confirmed when a deep, silver flank was exposed as the fish swirled in the margins, and moments later it came to the net.

Roach seem to vary a good deal from water to water; some are lean, insipid-looking creatures, but these Wharfe fish epitomise what a good river roach should be. They are invariably thick-backed, deep-flanked fish, often very plump and in many ways resembling a small carp in build. Their heads are small, the scales bronze-tinged and the fins the rich red of fresh blood. The fish grassed on that November evening had all the characteristics of a typical Wharfe roach; I weighed it at 1lb 7oz before slipping it into

45

a carp sack, which in my opinion is a much less damaging way of retaining a few small or middle-sized fish than a keepnet. These days I prefer not to retain fish at all, but I make an exception with roach because my experiences suggest that one spooked fish can easily disturb a whole shoal.

Within minutes of re-casting came another, identical bite, and the carbon curved against a fish which I knew from the moment the hook took hold to be another roach. The struggle suggested that this one was bigger, and that certainly appeared to be the case when I parted the wet meshes of the landing net. I thought that it might weigh close to 2lb, but the scales had other ideas and I eventually settled for 1lb 9oz.

It still wasn't properly dark as the swan shots plopped into the river for the third time. By now I was so involved with the fishing that the numbing breeze, which still rippled the surface, and the rain which spattered the umbrella, had almost been forgotten. The mallards were paddling in the margins a short distance downstream, waiting, as they often do at dusk, to move in and mop-up any tit-bits left behind upon my departure. I had no intention of leaving just yet, though.

The thin, white line of the quiver gave several sharp jags; I responded by sweeping the rod sideways and felt the thump of another hooked fish. It jigged about in mid-river for a few moments, then settled, hanging sullen and heavy in the gentle current. It felt bigger still as I coaxed it towards the bank. There were a few determined last ditch plunges in the margins, and some splashy swirls before the silver flank of another good roach broke through the surface reflections and was guided into the net. This one weighed 1¾lb.

Quite why the roach chose this day to go on a feeding spree remains a mystery, since to my way of thinking conditions were rather less than ideal, with the water still very cold following recent frosts. The fourth fish, another 1¾-pounder, joined the others in the carp sack. A glance at my watch revealed that it was not yet 5 o'clock; still less than an hour since I had switched to the quivertip. The final, and smallest roach of the evening at 1lb 1oz came shortly after the church bells in the nearby town had chimed the hour. Quite abruptly the feeding spell came to an end, and thereafter the quiver remained motionless. I tried introducing a little more mash, but to no avail; the evening's sport was over.

Subsequent visits to the river have not, as yet, found the roach in such suicidal mood again.

The big roach of the Wharfe are among the most unpredictable fish I have ever encountered. I still await my first 2-pounder from the river, and I shall continue to return in the hope of tempting one of these outsize specimens, for I've always enjoyed the challenge of difficult fish.

3   The Lagoon

The Lagoon is an enormous gravel pit of nearly 40 acres in extent, which was excavated quite recently, and consequently is rather bare and inhospitable in appearance. It is irregular in shape, and there are a number of interesting bays and promontories; similarly, the contours of the bottom vary considerably, with extensive shallows in some areas, while elsewhere the marginal shelf drops almost vertically down to 15 feet or more. Weed growth is luxuriant during the summer months; there are lush beds of Canadian pondweed in the margins, and a mantle of filamentous blanket weed over much of the pit's bottom. A few clusters of reeds have taken root in one or two sheltered areas at the southern end of the fishery, while the pure water promotes occasional heavy blooms of algae. On the uncultivated banks, a large variety of grassland plants flourish, and harbour a diversity of insect life, but tree cover is very sparse, restricted to a handful of wind-stunted hawthorns which are dotted around the water's edge.

In winter, when the skies are leaden and gales send white-capped waves rolling down the pit and crashing against the shingle, the Lagoon is a truly forbidding place. It was on such a day that I made my first visit to the fishery. I went in pursuit of pike, for which the pit has built up something of a reputation, but the driving rain forced me to retire early, damp, miserable and fishless. A couple more sessions that winter saw a solitary jack of a little over 4lb grassed, but it wasn't until the start of the new coarse-fishing season, the following June, that I began to fish the Lagoon in earnest. My good friend, Simon Linley, was a major influence in my decision to invest in a season permit for the fishery. He developed an infectious enthusiasm for the place after hearing tales about big bream, rudd, tench and carp, and we were making plans long before the season opened.

The last day of the close season was a fine one of warm sunshine, with hardly a breath of wind to ruffle the pit's surface. Mid-afternoon saw us both struggling beneath mountains of gear, as we made our way along the banks to our chosen swims. We both intended to fish from promontories at the mouths of large bays; Simon had been pre-baiting his swim for some days in advance, while I was hoping that a light baiting a few hours before the 'off' would be sufficient. We knew that the fishing would be difficult, but that anything we caught was likely to be of good size.

Arriving at my pitch, I began to tackle-up in leisurely fashion. I planned to use two rods, and decided to take advantage of my position on the promontory to place one bait in the mouth of the bay, and the other in the open pit. Plumbing revealed that in the bay, the margins shelved steeply down to a depth of 11 feet; I set up a match rod with a betalight float, in order to present a bait at the bottom of the slope. I planned to alternate between bread and sweetcorn baits, fished over a carpet of mashed bread and brown crumb. For the open pit, I chose a carbon Avon rod, and tackled-up to fish double maggot on a 14 hook, in combination with a swimfeeder. I groundbaited with a goodly quantity of hemp and maggots, bound together with a little brown crumb. An Optonic was used to give an audible bite indication, leaving me free to watch the float on the match rod.

With the swims groundbaited and the rods made up, I set about erecting my newly purchased Aquashed. I've got mixed feelings about bivvies; they are undoubtedly a boon for anglers who like to spend several days at the waterside, but to me, their presence on the bank is ugly and repelling. I succumbed to the temptation of buying one, however, because Simon and I were planning to spend a few two- and three-day sessions on the Lagoon.

By early evening everything was prepared, and all that remained to do was to pass time until midnight. Simon came round for a chat; neither of us had seen any signs of fish, save for a few jack pike in the margins. The deep, clear water looked promising, however, and there was an undercurrent of excitement in the air. Simon returned to his swim, leaving me alone to savour the atmosphere of the evening. All was still as darkness gradually began to descend; the honking of a distant flock of Canada geese carried across the pit, but no other sound broke the silence.

Midnight came, and within moments of casting out the two baits, a hint of a breeze sprang up. I expected it to drop again after a few minutes, but it didn't; in fact, it became a little stronger. It was an unpleasant, cold breeze, and it wasn't long before I retreated to the bivvy to shelter. Soon there was a quite substantial ripple on the water, and a heavy, swirling mist in the air. The wind caused the Optonic on the leger rod to give occasional, solitary bleeps, and these became more frequent during the course of the night as conditions deteriorated; a line clip would have solved the problem, but at the time I didn't possess such a thing. My confidence was evaporating and my eyes were beginning to feel heavy. I settled down to sleep, but before doing so I set the float rod on an old, antenna-type buzzer, so that there would be an audible warning should a bite occur. Not that I was expecting a bite in the fast worsening weather.

At some stage of the night the Optonic on the feeder rod gave three or four bleeps in quick succession, but by now the wind was quite wild and I had no reason to suspect a bite. I was more interested in sleeping than in fishing, and as I was feeling cold I decided to zip up the door of the Aquashed in order to keep out the wind. The rest of the night was passed in fitful sleep, until shortly after dawn, when I sensed a presence outside, and moments later somebody began to un-zip the door. It was Simon, looking tired and wind-blown. He reported three good bites and a number of twitches to legered breadflake, but unfortunately he had failed to hook anything. Most of this action had taken place shortly after midnight, when the weather was still reasonable.

When Simon returned to his tackle, I poked my head out of the door. It was a wild morning; damp mist was still swirling in the air, the water was grey and turbulent, and the wind was blowing rollers directly into the bay. The monkey climber indicator on the feeder rod had moved well up the stick, while the float on the match rod had drifted several feet, and was barely visible as it bobbed in the waves. I wound in both rods for bait checks, and was more than a little surprised to find that the maggots on the feeder tackle had been squashed to a pulp. I re-baited and re-filled the feeder, and punched the tackle back out into the waves. The occasional bleeps of the Optonic recommenced, until ten minutes later there was a sudden blur of sound, and in a flash I was at the rod. The tip bowed over as I struck, and for a brief moment I felt a solid resistance, before the hook pulled free. With my interest suddenly rejuvenated, I nicked a couple more lively maggots onto the hook and re-cast.

50

Quite suddenly, a heavy, driving rain came sweeping across the pit, and once more I was forced to retire to the bivvy. I soon began to feel tired again, and on the bed-chair I quickly drifted into sleep. I was grateful for the protection which the flapping Aqua-shed afforded from the wind and the beating rain. A drenched Simon awoke me again at 10am, although he had no more action to report. I told him about the happenings in my swim, and expressed the opinion that there might well have been a take on the feeder rod while I was asleep. I didn't fancy venturing out into the relentless wind and rain to find out, however. Simon wound in the feeder outfit for me, and sure enough, the maggots were pulped. I braved the elements for just long enough to replace the bait and re-cast, and then dived back into the bivvy with Simon.

We chatted for twenty minutes or so, before once again the Optonic bleeped several times in quick succession. Simon poked his head out of the door, and informed me that I had a bite, but I wasn't convinced. Despite this, I ventured out into the wind and rain to investigate, and as I moved towards the rod, the indicator began to crawl up the stick to the accompanying chatter of the Optonic. Once again I was into a solid fish, but as on the previous occasion, the line fell slack after a few moments, severed above the hook. No doubt the fish had swallowed the bait beyond its pharyngeal teeth, for I'm certain that I didn't apply enough pressure to cause the line to break.

There were no more bites on the feeder rod that morning. We spent a considerable amount of time discussing the two fish which had been lost, and trying to figure out the species. In the end we had to concede that the identity of those fish would probably always remain a mystery. The pulped maggots and the bite-off suggested a cyprinid species, however, and I was inclined to think that either tench or bream were the culprits. I was haunted by the thought that they might have been bream; the Lagoon's bream are few, but very large, and above all else it was the desire to tangle with them which had persuaded Simon and me to take out season permits.

Despite the fact that I had ventured out of the bivvy for only a few, brief moments, the dampness had penetrated, and I was feeling distinctly uncomfortable by the time the weather improved in the early afternoon. Although we had planned to fish for a couple of days, I wanted to return home for a hot bath and a change of clothes. Simon was like-minded, and so we packed up, vowing to return the following day.

Thinking back to that morning, the conditions were probably perfect (from the point of view of the fish) for my swim at the mouth of the bay. The wind was blowing directly towards the pitch, and I recall that the water in the margins was warm to the touch. No way was I going to face the driving rain in order to watch for bites, however. Had I been willing to do so, then perhaps I would have put a fish or two on the bank, and solved the mystery posed by the two lost fish.

Back again the following afternoon, I opted for the same swim and tactics, and put in a little more groundbait before starting. There was a moderate breeze blowing into the bay, and although there were one or two light showers, conditions were pleasant in comparison with the previous day. The only action before dark came to the feeder rod; I had seen no sign of a bite, but I decided to wind in for a bait check. When I attempted to do so, it appeared at first that I was snagged, but then came two sharp tugs, and the line fell slack. The hook came back bare.

At dusk the breeze dropped, and in the twilight I saw one or two tench roll, far across the bay, dark backs and big, round dorsal fins cleaving the surface. They were well out of fishing range, however. Before darkness set in, I dropped handfuls of sweetcorn into a couple of spots at the top of the marginal shelf, so that the yellow grains were plainly visible. I didn't intend to fish a bait among them, but I was interested to see if they were eaten during the night.

When it became properly dark, one or two heavy fish, which could only have been carp, began to crash out of the water on occasions, right in the margins where my betalight float glowed brightly. Twice the float dipped sharply, but both times the bait (sweetcorn) was rejected. Then all went quiet, and at a little after 1am, I put the float rod on the buzzer and retired to the bivvy to sleep. Apart from an abortive twitch on the feeder rod, I remained undisturbed until some time after 3am, when I was awoken abruptly by the buzzer on the float rod.

In my haste to get off the bed-chair I stumbled, and ended up crawling out of the bivvy on my hands and knees to reach the rod and strike. I connected with something which circled slowly in the margins, giving a few sullen thumps, as I struggled to regain composure and get to my feet. I suspected a tench, but when I finally sorted myself out and began to put a little pressure on the fish, I rapidly had cause to change my mind. It set off on a slow and deliberate run down the bay, and despite my attempts to restrain it, it just kept going and going. There must have been an enormous bow of line stretched across the water by the time the fish came to a halt, although of course I could see nothing in the darkness.

By now I was in no doubt about what I had hooked – it could only have been a carp. Gradually, it began to come back up the bay, and I slowly began to regain some of the line which I had been forced to yield. I thought that the fish had expended most of its energy on the first run, and I felt in control of the situation. But as I watched the silhouette of the rod tip against the dark sky, I became aware that the carp, far from yielding to pressure, had simply decided to run up the bay. Before long I was backwinding again as the fish headed for the open pit. This was bad news; a rusty metal pipe protrudes from the surface just a few yards out in the mouth of the bay. It is the only snag in the vicinity, to my knowledge, and the carp was getting perilously close. I piled on as much pressure as I dare with 4lb line, and for a moment the fish seemed to slow down, but then with a violent surge of power it thrust onwards. There was a grating sensation on the line; the carp had reached the pipe. It then stopped running quite suddenly, and began to yield. Suddenly the line fell slack. It hadn't parted, as I expected, but the hook-hold had given. I was choked.

Dawn was cold with a damp mist, and a light breeze which was blowing out of the bay. I noticed with interest that the sweetcorn which I had dropped into the margins the previous evening had all disappeared. Then I wound in the rods and set off, bleary-eyed, through the soaking grasses, heading for Simon's pitch to discuss the events of the night. He was hard fast asleep when I arrived; I woke him up and he stepped out into the chilly early morning air. His swim had been dead, and hadn't even produced a bite. I invited him to move round and share my swim, which, after some deliberation, he decided to do. We struggled along the banks with his gear, and he set up just a few yards down the bay from my position. After chatting for a while, we both retired for some sleep.

Our original plan had been to fish for just one night, but despite feeling tired, we both fancied stopping for a second night. At lunchtime, therefore, I headed for the nearby town to stock up on provisions and to buy fish and chips. We ate them on the bank, after which I tried to catch up on a little more lost sleep. I'm one of those people who needs lots of sleep, which is why I don't often fish long sessions. I find that on the first night of such a session I sleep little, but tiredness eventually catches up with me, after which I can't stay awake for more than an hour or so at a time. Far better, from my point of view, to fish single days or single nights, and to be in a fit state to respond when the action comes.

In mid-afternoon a buzzer sounded, and both Simon and myself stumbled eagerly out of our bivvies. My float-fished sweetcorn had been taken again, although this time by a lesser fish than that which had been hooked during darkness. It was quickly subdued, a rather manky 2½lb tench which surfaced in the wind-rippled water and was netted a few moments later. The remainder of the day, and the night which followed, passed without incident, much to our surprise and disappointment. I returned home the next morning, somewhat worse for the lack of sleep.

My fishing on the Lagoon during the remainder of the summer was of a rather more casual nature, restricted mainly to daytime and short after-work sessions. Nevertheless, both Simon and myself enjoyed good sport, in particular with rudd and tench. I was lucky enough to contact two of the elusive bream, specimens of 6lb 2oz and 6lb 10oz, nice fish but far from the largest in the pit.

Come August, small roach and perch began to show in increasing numbers, and it became difficult to sort out better fish from among them. In retrospect, we made a mistake by persevering with maggots; perhaps a change to a bait such as bread or sweetcorn would have brought better results.

I fished the Lagoon little during autumn and winter, but the following June I was back again, hoping that the knowledge gleaned during the first summer, coupled with a few new ideas, would bring about the downfall of more big fish. That second

Simon Linley bends into a double-figure carp

season, however, was a big disappointment; I caught a few reasonable fish, but blank sessions were numerous and this, along with the fact that others were achieving rather better results, caused my interest in the Lagoon to burn out. From the middle of August I fished elsewhere, and didn't visit the Lagoon again until the following season.

In trying to analyse why I had failed, I came to the conclusion that several aspects of my approach had been wrong. I had fished the Lagoon too often, on many occasions in circumstances which I knew from the outset offered little prospect of action; my fishing had taken place almost entirely during the daytime, whereas some night sessions might have paid dividends; and my choice of swims had been restricted largely to those which had produced the goods during my first season, when perhaps other areas of the pit were worth rather more attention than I had afforded to them.

Much of our success during the first season was achieved by fishing an extensive area of shallow water at the southern end of the pit, which often attracted fish during spells of warm weather. Fish were easy to locate in such conditions, and for the angler who chooses to tackle such a vast and thinly populated water, location is half the battle. One interesting thing which came to light during the second season was the discovery of two more large areas of shallow water, which were to figure in my fishing during my third summer on the Lagoon. But let me start at the beginning . . .

I missed opening day due to work, but the following day I arrived at the pit to find conditions looking perfect, bright and warm with just a light breeze rippling the southern shallows. The new reed growth was just beginning to push through, but as yet the fresh green blades had still not reached the height of the brown, shrivelled remnants of the previous year's growth. Weed, too, was rather sparse; the sandy bed was exposed over large areas of the shallows, whereas by the end of June the bottom would be hidden by a thick mantle of green.

I elected to fish from a sandbank which shelves gently into the water, adjacent to a reedbed. I catapulted out a little sweetcorn; the yellow grains remained plainly visible on the sun-illuminated flats, at least when the surface was calm, during lulls in the breeze. Carp were in evidence, several of them, dark shadows drifting beneath the ripple. From time to time one of them would

A fine brace of rudd

move over the corn and mop up a few grains, before passing on. I fished for them, even missed a couple of takes, but eventually spoilt my chances by re-casting too frequently, chasing the fish instead of waiting for them to find the bait. Carp remained in the area, but now the corn was ignored.

I turned my attention to a handful of rudd which I'd spotted hanging in pockets of open water among the reeds. Crouching, I waded slowly through the stalks, until I was close enough to lower a maggot-baited hook into one of the clear pools. The bait vanished, the strike failed to connect and the fish melted into the growth. A little more careful wading and I re-located them, repeated the procedure and watched a bronze form glide up to and intercept the slowly sinking maggot. It splashed and swirled until the line became entwined among the stalks and a broad, golden flank lay tantalisingly exposed on the surface. A little careful prodding and pushing with the landing net saw the rudd safely enveloped in the meshes, and I splashed back to the bank.

It was a familiar fish, the torn top lip and a slight scale deformation on the left flank identifying it as one I had caught on two occasions during the previous summer, both times from the same area of the pit. Rudd, of course, are very nomadic fish, but I wonder if different shoals have their own territory within a water? It seems that a certain, small group of fish are the ones which invariably occupy this reedy corner of the Lagoon when conditions are suitable. For the third time I recorded the weight of the fish at 1lb 10oz, a rudd which had seemingly reached the limit of its growth.

I failed to add to the catch, the remainder of the shoal having vanished; nevertheless, a most encouraging start to the season, I felt. Determined not to make last year's mistake of forsaking everything for the Lagoon, I made a dawn start on a tench pool the following day. When activity diminished as the sun climbed above the tree tops, however, I decided to pack my tackle and head for the Lagoon, with conditions again looking ideal.

The breeze on this occasion was a little stronger, pushing quite a heavy ripple into the reeds. Fish were present again, both rudd and carp, and mostly they seemed to be active within the confines of the rushes. I decided to tackle the rudd first, and managed to hook two of them, but pulled out of both as they splashed and plunged among the stalks; thereafter, I saw not a sign of rudd, but carp remained in evidence.

I tackled up a carbon Avon rod, threading 8lb line through the eyes and tying a number 8 hook to the business end. Bait was a single grain of sweetcorn, and a couple of BB shot nipped onto the line aided control in the breeze. The carp seemed to favour a certain corner among the rushes; several sizeable, blue-backed fish were basking in the sun's warmth, this despite quite considerable surface movement caused by the wind. I waded carefully through the growth, until I was close enough to lower the corn to one of the fish; its reaction was to turn away, push through the stalks and settle a little further on. I repeated the procedure, on quite a number of occasions, without tempting a fish, yet neither did I scare them away. In fact, they were amazingly tolerant of my presence, simply shifting positions when I lowered a bait before them and sometimes emerging to bask between the rod tip and myself! Once or twice fish bolted, jostling the stalks and leaving a billow in the water, but within a minute or two they would drift back into the rushes to bask again. Most extraordinary behaviour.

As time passed the carp seemed to become increasingly suspicious, and began to drift in and out of the rushes. Every now and then one would move close enough for me to offer a bait, and now I noticed another strange quirk in their behaviour; it seemed that they were beginning to take an interest in the corn. Surface movement made it hard to follow their actions at times, but on several occasions I thought I saw the corn sucked in and quickly ejected as it sank.

There were periods now, short ones of a minute or two, when the rushes were devoid of carp, but odd fish kept returning. Then I saw two fish, which I estimated at about 10lb apiece, push through the stalks mere feet from where I stood, and I immediately lowered a grain of sweetcorn in front of the leader. It moved forward and sucked in the bait at once. I struck instantly, for fear that the corn might be ejected; there was a heavy crash, and the rod buckled round. I had to back-wind quickly as the fish furrowed through the sparse growth, a bow-wave in its wake and the cracking and rustling of the old, yellow-brown stalks quite audible. It didn't go far, and began to flounder and wallow when it reached the outermost stalks; the line had become entwined amongst the growth, which effectively cushioned the efforts of the fish to move further away. I managed to regain a few turns of line, but thereafter the carp became quite firmly stuck, wedged among the reeds with its back out of water, its bronze, fully scaled flank plainly visible.

Well, I had no intention of losing this fish for the sake of keeping my feet dry, so after reaching round for the landing net, I began to wade out towards it. The sudden, cold sensation of water gushing over the tops of my boots caused me to gasp, but I squelched on until the carp was within netting range. It made a last-ditch surge, but was soon worked back to the clump of stalks around which the line had tangled. I had some difficulty in getting it into the net, since my prodding and lifting tended to push the clump of reeds away and these, in turn, pulled the fish with them. After much careful manoeuvring, though, I finally had a great pig of a common carp in the meshes, whereupon I broke the line above the hook and struggled back ashore.

Although I had estimated the fish at 10lb when I saw it take the bait, it was clear upon seeing its enormous belly that it was much heavier. In fact, the scales swung round to 19lb 9oz. I lowered it, still in the net, into the margins while I emptied my boots and prepared the camera to take a few photographs. After returning the fish I decided to call it a day and head for home.

As you can imagine, after my dismal results during the previous season I was quite enthralled with this early success. Even so, I was determined not to fall into a rut with my fishing on the Lagoon, and thus I chose once again to make a dawn start on a different water the following day. If conditions looked right, I reasoned, I could always pack my tackle and head for the Lagoon in mid-morning.

As it happened, conditions on that day looked far from right. The early morning was cool, grey and breezy, and I spent it struggling for bites on a lily-choked woodland pool. By 10am, further fishing seemed futile, so I tackled down and packed my gear into the car. I decided to stop at the Lagoon on the way home; I didn't plan to fish, but I wanted a look round.

I was surprised, upon arriving, to find that the breeze had dropped and the pit was calm, just lightly ruffled on occasions. I was even more surprised, in view of the grey skies and the cool air temperature, when my observations revealed a few rudd among the reeds. Without further ado, I unloaded the tackle from the car and prepared to fish for them. Unfortunately, despite my stealthy approach, the fish seemed to sense my presence and had disappeared by the time I found myself in a position to lower a bait into the pool where they had been lying. I continued to wade cautiously through the stalks, scanning the water carefully, knowing that I hadn't created enough disturbance to drive the rudd out of the vicinity. After fifteen minutes of futile searching, though, I was beginning to think that perhaps they had indeed departed. I was standing among the outermost stalks, and a few feet ahead of me, motionless on the edge of the reeds, was a tiny jack pike of 6 inches long. I decided to drop my maggot in front of it. No sooner had I done so than I saw two bronze shapes approaching swiftly through the shallow water; one of them turned, glided up to the

A big carp safely netted

maggot and sipped it in. There was a flurry and a swirl as the hook sunk home, and thereafter the rudd struggled determinedly, plunging repeatedly, exposing a gleaming, golden flank as it rolled across the surface. Stumbling back through the stalks, I guided the fish across the sandy shallows until I was able to reach the net.

While the rudd was by no means untidy in appearance, in fact it was generally in good shape, it had what I can best describe as a 'nearly new' look which suggested that perhaps this was not the first time it had felt a hook. It weighed 1½lb.

Two consecutive dawn starts had left me feeling quite tired, and I was now ready to dismantle my tackle and return home. However, another of the Lagoon's regular anglers, who was fishing from a bivvy a little further along the bank, ambled round for a chat; the conversation lasted some time, during which a light breeze began to ruffle the surface and I noticed that the temperature was increasing appreciably. As we chatted, my friend pointed to a dark shape beneath the ripple, and not far from where we stood. 'Is that a carp?' he asked. I wasn't sure, but as we watched I became increasingly convinced that it was. Soon, all doubt was removed when it slowly turned and drifted away, until surface glare and ripple hid it from view. As we continued to chat, there was a heavy swirl out over the flats. Despite my tiredness, I knew that this was an opportunity I couldn't ignore.

Pulling my carbon Avon rod from the holdall, I threaded 6lb line through the eyes and tied on a number 12 hook. A 2AAA link-leger provided just enough weight to punch a single grain of sweetcorn about 20 yards out into the ripple. I placed the rod in rests and squeezed a bread bobbin onto the line, between the reel and the butt ring, before catapulting a couple of pouchfuls of corn into the vicinity of the hookbait.

An occasional heavy crash or swirl betrayed the fact that there were now one or two sizeable fish in the area. To add to the excitement, there was a sudden sharp jerk of the bobbin, which I took to be caused by a fish swimming into the line. A little later, the bobbin moved unsteadily towards the butt ring; I struck at thin air, and hastily wound in to re-bait, unsure if it was just another liner or if I'd missed a take.

For a short while, sunshine filtered through the cloud, the breeze dropped away and the surface fell calm. In the baited area

I could make out several dark shapes, moving slowly, almost imperceptibly, over the sandy bed of the pit. I had a feeling that one or two tench might be moving among the carp, but the fish were too far away to identify with certainty. A ripple had sprung up again when the bread bobbin gave a sudden 6-inch jerk, and then slid swiftly towards the butt ring. I swept the rod over my shoulder, half expecting to miss again, but just before it reached the vertical I felt the hook make impact. The fish reacted instantly with a surge of violent power, and I had to lower the rod tip abruptly for fear of a smash. For a while the carp seemed bewildered, and made a couple of short lunges in the direction of the thick bank of reeds in the margins to my left. Then it turned and ran heavily over the flats, the line cutting through and lifting from the water in its wake, picking up a few threads of weed which hung like washing from the large bow stretched across the shallows. After travelling some distance the fish slowed and I began to regain line; sometimes the dark back and erect dorsal fin of the carp lifted through the surface.

It seemed that it was all over when, in a final flurry, the carp turned and lumbered into the reeds, where it wallowed and became stuck among the outermost stalks. I had my waders on, so rather than take a risk by trying to bully it free, I picked up the net and began to paddle out, pausing every few yards to give the reel a few turns and retain a tight line. As I neared the fish, a good mirror which I could see wedged against a clump of stalks, it gave a frantic thrust and broke free from the rushes which had tethered it. By now, though, its energy had been sapped, and it could only flounder weakly on the surface as I guided it into the net. It was a short, solid fish, with tiny scales scattered along the flanks and extraordinary, large paddle-like fins. It weighed 13¾lb, and after wading out a short way to find water deep enough to enable it to swim away, I was more than happy to allow a friend, who had arrived for an evening session, to take over the swim while I returned home for an early night.

The next day the weather broke, remaining unsettled for the best part of two weeks, and the fish disappeared from the shallows. Then came another day of hot sunshine; unfortunately I had to spend it working, but my tackle was in the car and when I finished,

This solid mirror carp weighed an ounce short of 17lb

I headed straight to the Lagoon for an evening session. By the time that I arrived, however, the sky had clouded over and light rain had started to fall. It continued to rain intermittently throughout the evening, but fortunately not heavily enough to necessitate setting up an umbrella. Furthermore, the air remained warm, and things looked promising as I tackled up.

I'd selected a swim in one of the shallow areas which had come to light during the previous season. There is a large bay on the east bank of the pit, along one side of which the depth averages 3 feet. My pitch had been selected more or less at random in this area. During hot weather, particularly if a breeze is blowing into the bay, as it was on the day in question, fish often move into these shallows. I saw nothing at first, but at some stage during preparations I stood up abruptly; there was a heavy billow in the margins, just a few yards out, and I saw the dark form of a sizeable carp glide away, soon to be lost to sight beneath the reflections. Most encouraging.

Two rods were assembled: with one I planned to fish a double-maggot bait on float tackle, and with the other, a grain of sweetcorn on a 2-swan-shot link-leger. First cast on sweetcorn, there

64

was a heavy pull as the bait sank; I waited a few moments, but nothing further happened. As I took up slack, however, there came a sudden tenseness in the line. I struck instantly, felt the hook bite and glimpsed the pale gleam of a flank beneath the lightly rippled surface. A moment later the line fell slack, bitten through just above the hook. On reflection, I think that a fish took the bait on the drop, then moved towards me, so that contact was lost for a while; by the time the strike was made, the hook had been swallowed beyond the pharyngeal teeth, and a bite-off followed.

Thereafter, a fine, filamentous weed which coated large areas of the bottom caused difficulties; after casting out the leger tackle, sinking the line and tightening up, there was a nagging worry that the corn might have become buried. To overcome this I changed to a float, bunching the shot beneath it and fishing overdepth, which enabled me to sink the line immediately after casting, leaving the bait to fall on a slack line and, hopefully, settle upon the weed. So, with two black-tipped floats riding the ripple, and loose feed catapulted around both, I settled down to await events.

There was an abundance of pike activity during the course of the evening; on several occasions, jacks followed the baits into the margins as I retrieved them. Once, as I drew a float across the surface moments after casting, it was attacked in a heavy and violent swirl which appeared to be caused by a sizeable fish. Pike were not my quarry, however, and I took much more interest when, at around 7.30pm, the float on the corn-baited outfit gave a strong dip. I sat up in my chair, hovering over the rod in anticipation, and sure enough, a few moments later, the black tip sank slowly into the ripple. Sweeping the rod round, I made contact with a cumbersome-feeling fish which hugged the bottom, moving slowly and without any real purpose. It soon began to yield and I guided it towards the margins, where it made a short, heavy rush, bow-waving through the shallow water. As it turned, the dark back and large, round dorsal fin of a big tench broke the surface. Thereafter, the resistance was minimal, and moments later a spawn-filled fish came wallowing over the rim of the net, the hook falling from its mouth as the meshes folded around it.

I knew, as I lifted the net and lay it among the damp bankside grasses, that this was the largest tench I had ever caught. It was a typical gravel-pit fish, in pristine condition, with not a blemish of any description on its glistening, green body. Although carrying spawn, it was by no means bloated or mis-proportioned. I thought that it might weigh as much as 7lb, but the scales settled a few ounces short of that figure at 6lb 11oz.

The remainder of the evening was spent in something of a trance, and I failed to add to the catch. Carp and tench remained in evidence, betrayed by an occasional heavy crash or swirl within the confines of the bay, but often some distance away from the area which I was fishing. There was one further moment of excitement when the maggot float vanished; a split second later there was a violent swirl on the surface, exactly where the float had been. I struck at thin air, and upon retrieving the tackle, found that the hooklength had parted. The fish involved, I suspect, was a pike, but I can offer no explanation for this strange happening.

The third extensive shallow area is situated on the west side of the Lagoon; cattle which graze the adjoining field frequently drink here, paddling into water which is a fairly even 2 feet in depth. In hot weather these shallows are much frequented by carp, often in considerable numbers. When the surface is calm, their dark forms can be distinguished, slipping like shadows over the thick weed which carpets the bottom; in a ripple, they are betrayed by occasional heavy crashes or swirls, or bow-waves as they move across the flats. I have seen bream here, too; usually they glide past in small groups, perhaps a couple of average sized fish of 6 or 7lb, often accompanied by a monster which might weigh 8lb or more. The Lagoon's bream remain something of a mystery, for despite fairly frequent sightings, they are caught rarely; during the course of an average season, the number which are landed can be counted on the fingers of two hands.

These shallows have always proved very difficult to fish, due to the dense and very soft weed which invariably covers the bottom during the summer months. It is all too easy for baits and loose feed to sink into this mantle of green and become hidden, a situation which can be very frustrating when fish are constantly active in the vicinity. Of course, weed can be a problem in the two aforementioned shallow areas, but neither boast such thick, dense growth as the Cattle-Drink Shallows. Perhaps it is the cattle which hold the key to this situation, their dung adding to the fertility of the pit's bed.

I fished the Cattle-Drink Shallows on several occasions during the latter half of June and throughout July, but my results were not as good as they should have been, considering the number of fish which were present at times. Clearly, I needed to devise some means of keeping baits above the weed. One of the ideas which I tried was to use suspended maggots; maggots can be made to float by dropping them into a bait box with a shallow filling of water, which should not be of sufficient depth to immerse the grubs. After ten to fifteen minutes, they will be ready. Some maggots seem to float better than others, but generally two of them will be buoyant enough to support a forged number 16 hook. I fished the bait on float tackle, with a BB shot, which was positioned 6 inches from the hook, resting on the bottom, so that the maggots were suspended above the weed.

Of course, floating maggots were of no use as feed, so I simply catapulted undoctored bait into the swim on a little and often basis. However, I knew that the loose maggots would quickly bury into the soft weed, and so as something extra to attract fish I decided to throw a couple of handfuls of mashed bread, stiffened with a little brown crumb, around the float. This, I hoped, would flake and cloud through the water to spread across and partially sink into the weed. Only a few carp were evident on the day in question , but I was encouraged by the capture of a sleek, though rather small mirror. It weighed just less than 7lb, and was, I believe, one of a batch of stock fish which were released a couple of years previously.

In late July I arrived at the Lagoon for an after-work session on a blazing hot afternoon. The breeze was a very light easterly, perfect for the Cattle-Drink Shallows, which is where I headed. Approaching the swim through a profuse growth of ragwort which set the field ablaze with yellow, I deposited the tackle and then crept towards the water's edge, crouching low and scanning the ripple for signs of fish. As I drew near, the surface erupted in a heavy swirl, just a few feet from the bank, and moments later the shuddering form of a big mirror carp rose from the water, dark back glistening in the sunshine before it crashed back.

It was one of those occasions when I couldn't tackle up quickly enough; keeping well back from the water's edge, I fumbled badly in my attempts to thread 6lb line through the eyes of the carbon Avon. In the end all was prepared, and I crept very quietly to the water's edge to position items such as rod rests, landing net and chair. Every now and then came another heavy crash, and I'd look round to see a calm patch spreading in the ripple.

I had obtained a block of foamed polystyrene, from which I detached a small piece and sandwiched it on a number 12 hook, between two kernels of sweetcorn. Thus the bait was made to float, and could be suspended above the weed by using a BB shot as an anchor. A Driftbeater float completed the outfit, the tip painted a uniform black as I find that this colour shows up well on extensive waters, when viewed against a background of reflected sky.

As I attempted to cast out there was a loud crack, and the rod literally collapsed in my hands. A weak point in the carbon, just above the butt, had given and caused the rod to fold in two. Cursing under my breath, not least because this meant a further delay before I could start fishing, I dismantled the tackle and transferred the reel to the only other rod which I had available. This was a 14-feet-long carbon, described by the maker as a match rod, but in my opinion not really suited to the light lines generally used in match fishing. I find it ideal for float fishing with lines in the three to four pound breaking strain range, when species such as tench, bream or chub are the quarry. With 6lb line it was perhaps overloaded, but in the circumstances I had no alternative.

A few minutes later I was ready, and I tip-toed back to the water's edge. A short, diagonal cast to the right dropped the bait about 10 feet from the bank, in an area where I had recently observed some surface movement. Placing the rod in rests, I prepared to catapult a little loose feed into the vicinity. Due to the shallow water, I decided to introduce just four or five grains of sweetcorn at a time, so as not to disturb fish which might be in close proximity. As the first few grains spattered the surface, the water billowed; one carp, it seemed, had already been spooked, so I decided to refrain from introducing more feed for a short while.

Two or three minutes passed, and with no further evidence of fish in the immediate vicinity of the float, I risked catapulting a few more grains of corn. Nothing happened to suggest that I'd disturbed anything else, so I catapulted a little more, and then settled to wait. After a few more minutes came a gentle humping of the surface, just a short distance away from the float, as if a carp had up-ended over the feed. I waited, watching the black tip ride the ripple. Suddenly, it vanished. Sweeping the rod round, I made contact, a violent swirl indicating that the fish had already travelled a few yards, sensing that something was amiss even before I struck. With the flimsy carbon well hooped, I had to yield line quickly as the carp set off on a long, heavy rush across the flats. Soon, though, it slowed, held back not only by my own efforts to apply pressure, but also by the soft folds of weed which accumulated on the line, and hung in some quantity from the large bow which stretched across the surface. I began to regain line slowly, the ponderous, heavy movements of the carp exaggerated by the considerable weight of weed. Soon I had it in the margins where there was a final flurry, a few heavy swirls and short plunges, the golden-orange flank of a good mirror illuminated by the sunlight as the fish turned and rolled. It was netted with difficulty, as the water before me was so shallow that the fish almost became grounded.

It was a very beautiful carp, sleek and dark, the back a rich chocolate-brown, tinted with purple, giving way to orange on the flanks and fading to an amber belly. Setting up camera, tripod and air cable, I posed with the fish for a few photographs against a backdrop of ragwort. Then I waded out to find water deep enough to release the carp. It weighed 14lb.

While this run of success with the Lagoon's carp was most welcome, the fact remained that I wanted to catch bream above all else. It was becoming increasingly apparent that the two landed during my first season were lucky fish, and by now it was clear that short daytime sessions were unlikely to produce another. A positive approach was needed if success was to be achieved. With three weeks' holiday due in August, I determined to spend a few nights on the Lagoon.

For the first of these night sessions, I chose the pitch which I fished during that wild first morning of the season, two years previously. Since those early days on the Lagoon I had neglected the Pipe Swim, but now I found myself puzzling over the two fish lost on the opening morning. I wondered if, by adopting the same tactics, I could find out if they were, as I suspected, bream.

The chosen night was cool, grey and rather breezy. There was

A pristine Lagoon tench

no action during darkness, but the following morning a tench of 5lb 6oz and a mirror carp of 12lb 1oz fell to maggot/caster cocktail, fished in combination with a swimfeeder. While the results of the session were pleasing in that two nice fish were grassed in unfavourable conditions, I was nevertheless no nearer to catching a bream. There was, of course, no firm evidence to suggest that the Pipe Swim was likely to produce a bream, but it was still too early to write it off, and in the absence of other likely areas I decided to try there again on my next visit.

Most modern literature devoted to the pursuit of large still-water bream centres around the location of patrol routes and feeding areas; finding these, by all accounts, is half the battle. The Lagoon is so vast, and so thinly populated by the species, though, that I found it almost impossible to track the fish down. Of course, I had sighted them in various places and I knew a number of swims from which they had been caught. Usually, though, these sightings and catches had taken place in conditions of hot weather, when the bream had probably ventured far away from their main feeding areas. Neither could surface activity be used as a guide to the movements of the fish, since I had never seen bream rolling or priming in the Lagoon. Other anglers seemed interested mainly in the carp and pike, so I was fishing alone and to a large extent blindly, trying to piece together the scant information which was available. I felt sure that there would be places,

70

perhaps confined areas of certain swims which, if discovered, would produce bream with something approaching consistency.

Another dilemma centred around the groundbait; in particular, the ingredients and the quantity needed to achieve the best results. It is my belief that the Lagoon's bream usually move in small groups of two, three or four fish. Working on this assumption, it was necessary to find a balance between introducing insufficient feed to hold the fish in the swim, and introducing feed of a composition or in a quantity that would fill them before they took the hookbait. Casters and hemp I regarded as essential ingredients, since both will hold bream in an area and keep them foraging, each fish capable of consuming a considerable number of these tiny particles. Stewed wheat was used too, though I'm not sure if it had any beneficial effect. Bread, while an additional attraction, was likely to fill the fish quickly. Therefore I opted for just a solitary loaf, stiffened with the appropriate amount of brown crumb; this made a useful binding agent into which to mix the particles, the resultant blend being of a good, throwable consistency. Of course, it was always likely that my baiting schemes would be upset by the appearance of tench or carp in the swim, but such hazards I can live with!

On my next session in the Pipe Swim, I decided to stay for two nights. Having spent the day working, I arrived on a Friday evening with just two hours left before nightfall. The first job was to erect the bivvy, after which I mixed and introduced the groundbait, before turning my attention to the tackle. By now I had obtained a replacement Avon rod, and this was rigged to fish a maggot/caster cocktail in combination with a swimfeeder, in the baited area. With the second rod, I planned to fish sweetcorn amongst a smattering of loose offerings in the margins of the bay, in the hope of tempting tench or carp.

The light had faded almost completely by the time I was prepared, the first stars visible in a cloudless sky, and the cool south-westerly breeze had dropped to leave the Lagoon's surface flat calm. One or two fish gave clearly audible swirls, out in the mouth of the bay. Soon I retired to the sleeping bag, in which I lay gazing out of the bivvy door. Sometimes I'd catch a fleeting glimpse of the dark smudge of a bat against the night sky. The distant barking of a dog carried across the becalmed pit from a farm on the far side; eventually the dog settled, and I saw the lights of the farmhouse go out. I slept fitfully, as I always do when fishing, disturbed on several occasions by short, sharp bursts from the Optonics, which were caused, I think, by bats flying into the lines.

When dawn eventually broke, bright, warm and calm, there had still been no bites. At breakfast time a cool breeze began to ruffle the surface again, and it gradually became stronger, until by mid-afternoon a heavy chop was pushing down the pit. There was a possible take during the morning, when I retrieved the feeder outfit having seen no indication of a bite, and found just a shelled caster remaining on the hook.

I don't treat long sessions lightly, and I indulge in them only when circumstances suggest that they are necessary. Having fished for the best part of twenty-four hours for just one, possible bite, I found my interest beginning to wane, and for a period during the afternoon I contemplated returning home. Only the thought of the time and bait already invested in the session persuaded me to stay, rather than give up with nothing to show for my efforts.

For the second night, I decided to abandon the margin-fished sweetcorn, and instead rig up the rod to fish breadcrust in combination with a swimfeeder, in the groundbaited area. A BB shot, nipped onto the line just a couple of inches from the hook, ensured that the crust would remain close to the bottom. The tips of both rods were submerged in order to avoid false bites caused by bats.

The night was again uneventful, and I awoke to a pleasant, bright dawn, with just the lightest of easterly breezes pushing out of the bay, ruffling the surface in places but leaving large areas calm. I replaced both baits and re-cast, before returning to the sleeping bag, where I gradually drifted into sleep.

Suddenly I was awoken by the steady tone of an Optonic, as something bolted with the maggot/caster cocktail. Grabbing the rod, I realised at once that I'd contacted another carp. It ran hard, far out into the pit, while I simply held the rod high, allowing the reel handle to revolve freely as I struggled to pull my boots on. The fish was still running by the time I got to my feet, but shortly afterwards it reached a weedbed, and all movement ceased. A large bow of line hung across the surface, and only when it was stretched close to breaking point did there come a strange, jerking sensation as stalks began to sever. Soon a thick, green tangle broke the surface, cleaving a gentle furrow as I pulled it towards the bank. Although at this stage I could feel nothing of the fish, I noticed that the weed was cutting to the left a little as I wound. Presently, the knot of stalks and leaves reached the margins, and I pulled it away in big, dripping handfuls, flinging it aside until the line was clear. Then I wound down until I regained contact with the fish, which had moved left and was still far out in the pit.

For a while, it moved ponderously in open water, sometimes cutting a gentle bow wave as it cruised close to the surface. Almost unwittingly, I had moved down the shingle to get nearer. Before long I had the fish on a short line; it worked slowly along the margins, wallowing tantalisingly on the surface on several occasions, as if almost beaten. From these glimpses I knew that I'd hooked a sizeable common carp. I followed it to the mouth of the bay, where it surfaced again over the deeps beyond the steep marginal drop-off, dark back glistening in the early morning sunshine. Crouching low, I gently submerged the net and applied a little extra pressure in an effort to coax the carp over the rim.

Suddenly the fish panicked, swirled violently and surged away, leaving the surface rocking. The reel handle span again as line vanished rapidly from the spool. Only when the carp drew close to the opposite side of the bay did it slow, before turning and following the far bank for a short distance. Gradually, it began to cut across, until eventually it lumbered into the thick, overhanging grasses further down the bay to my right. Following several heavy swirls among the trailing stalks, the fish yielded and allowed me to guide it up the margin. This time when it surfaced beneath the rod tip, the fight was at an end.

As with the carp landed during the previous session, the struggle had lasted almost exactly half an hour. This fish, however, was considerably larger, and I considered myself lucky to have landed it on 3lb line and a number 16 hook. It weighed 18lb 5oz, and was still carrying spawn, a little of which dripped from the vent when I held the fish for photographs.

Two tench were landed later in the morning, one each to maggot/caster cocktail and breadcrust. Both were females, weighing 5lb 2oz and 4¾lb, and both were carrying spawn. The Lagoon is so large, deep and exposed, that a sustained spell of hot weather is needed in order to produce suitable conditions for fish to spawn. Such conditions, it seemed, had simply not occurred during the summer in question, when the weather was exceptionally cool, wet and windy. Having failed to spawn by mid-August, it is doubtful that the fish would have found opportunity to do so during the remainder of the summer. Thus their spawn would have been re-absorbed during the autumn and winter, resulting in the loss of a whole year class of fish. This is not such a disaster as it might appear, for on a water such as the Lagoon, the very poor survival rate of fry is one of the factors which enables the few fish which reach adulthood to grow so well, thriving on the lack of competition for food.

By the time the second of those tench was landed, the sky had greyed over and rain was slanting down on the easterly wind. With conditions worsening I decided that enough was enough; an hour later, tackle packed into the car, I headed for home, tired and sodden, but happy.

With still no evidence of bream, I decided that my next session would be spent in a different swim. I chose a promontory, across the mouth of the bay from the Pipe Swim, partly because I knew that a bream of 7lb 9oz had been caught there early in the season. This fish had fallen to a carp angler who was now concentrating his efforts elsewhere on the Lagoon, so I knew that there would be no ill feeling when I moved into his old pitch. Another two-night stay was planned, and the day before I intended to start I decided to visit the Lagoon, in order to plumb the swim and introduce some groundbait.

The location of the swim is interesting in that it is situated directly opposite a gravel promontory on the far side of the pit; thus a bottleneck is formed between the broad north and south ends of the Lagoon. Even here, the distance from bank to bank is in excess of a hundred yards, but it seemed that this might be a good place to intercept fish as they moved from one area of the pit to another.

A sunken gravel spit protrudes just a short distance into the swim; it has a shallow covering of water and is cloaked by a mantle of fine, filamentous weed. Beyond the spit, and on both sides, the bottom shelves away steeply to a depth of 12 feet. While plumbing the swim, a random cast with the float set at 8 feet revealed a plateau some 30 yards out, the sort of feature which in my

Fruits of a long session: tench of 5lb 2oz and 4¾lb dwarfed by an 18lb 5oz common carp

experience is often attractive to bream. Leaving the float out as a marker, I threw in the groundbait, a task made difficult by the distance involved and by a facing wind. The end result was that feed was scattered over a wide area. Nevertheless, I departed with the feeling that I was a step closer to the long awaited big bream.

The following day was a fine one of warm sunshine, with just a very light breeze ruffling the surface of the pit on occasions. Arriving at the pitch in early afternoon, I set about tackling up, this time electing to fish two feeder outfits right from the start, one baited with maggot/caster cocktail, the other with crust. I used an inflatable rubber dinghy in order to introduce groundbait, rowing out to a marker float with a bucketful of mashed bread, to which casters, hemp, stewed wheat and a few maggots were added. With everything prepared, I cast out the baits and sat back to enjoy the sunshine, expecting nothing until nightfall.

Following the disturbance caused by using the dinghy, I was most surprised when a fish swirled heavily, just a short distance to my right and not far from the bank. Several sizeable carp were in

75

evidence, betrayed occasionally by vortices in the water, or by dark nebs which sometimes pushed through the surface. Gradually the fish drifted away, out into the pit, ignoring the loose crusts which I catapulted into their path. I have yet to see one of the Lagoon's carp take a floating bait.

Late in the afternoon a very large bird of prey flew over the pit, high up and far away, mobbed by a couple of gulls which were dwarfed by comparison. I remain mystified as to its identity, and can only guess that it was either a rare vagrant such as a white-tailed eagle, or an escapee from a zoo.

At dusk, the sky clouded a little and a cool breeze sprang up. Sedge flies were evident in abundance, as they invariably are during summer evenings on the Lagoon. Dozens of these moth-like insects had settled on the outside of the bivvy, while the first bats were hawking across the surface to intercept those which were still airborne. In the half-light, there came a sudden, short trill from one of the Optonics. It was the crust-baited outfit; the monkey was dangling precariously at the top of the stick, but all movement had ceased before I reached the rod. I struck, more in hope than in any real expectation of hooking a fish, but I was pleasantly surprised to make contact with something. For a few seconds it hung deep, then it yielded quite easily, swirling over the weed at the outermost edge of the gravel spit, the pale gleam of a broad flank visible for a fleeting moment in the gloaming. Wallowing and plunging, a good rudd was hustled across the shallows and into the net.

Perhaps it is because these fish are so scarce that I gain such pleasure from their capture; even the Lagoon's carp and tench do not compare, as far as I'm concerned, with a sizeable rudd. This one weighed 1lb 13oz, a rather old-looking fish, slightly tarnished in appearance.

In darkness the breeze dropped away, and during the early hours of the morning a heavy mist descended over the pit. At some stage of the night there came another bite, a slow 6-inch twitch to the maggot/caster cocktail, which failed to develop further. Retrieving the tackle, I found just a squashed maggot remaining on the hook. After re-baiting, I could do nothing more than cast blindly into the greyness, and hope that the tackle had splashed down in the right area.

Dawn was just a gradual transformation, light seeping slowly through the grey wall of mist outside the bivvy door. Later, a cool breeze began to ruffle the surface, and thereafter the mist gradually lifted, but the sky remained grey and sombre throughout the following day. A number of showers came sweeping across the pit, spattering the rippled surface; long periods were spent by necessity in the confines of the bivvy, and once again I realised how monotonous a long session on the Lagoon can be.

It became evident that the plateau was coated in parts by a thin layer of filamentous weed; from time to time a little would be found draped over the maggot/caster cocktail when I retrieved the tackle. This was an undesirable situation, so I changed to two floating maggots and nipped a BB shot onto the line, a couple of inches from the hook. Thus both baits were suspended above the bottom. It wasn't long before the double maggot was taken by a perch of 1lb 13oz, which was the only action during the day.

Dusk came early, light seeping from the cloudy sky. When it was almost dark, I missed another fast take on maggot, striking at thin air and retrieving a bare hook. Shortly afterwards, the cool south-easterly breeze, which had moderated during the course of the evening, dropped away to leave the pit flat calm. In the gloaming, the sound of a heavy swirl broke the silence; I peered out from the bivvy door, and vaguely distinguished ripples spreading across the surface, directly above the baited area. A little later it happened again, and in the pale, orange glow of light from the nearby town, I saw another vortex over the swim. Then an Optonic chattered, the monkey twitched a few inches up the stick, and stopped. I waited a few moments, but nothing further happened, so I retrieved the tackle to check the maggots, which were unmarked.

Tiredness was beginning to creep over me, following a limited amount of sleep during the previous night. I retired to the sleeping bag, but thoughts of rest were quickly dispelled by three or four bleeps from an Optonic, this time to the crust-baited outfit. Line bites? It seemed likely; I pulled the monkey back down to its original position and waited, wondering if the crust was still intact. A few minutes later, the monkey twitched up a few inches again, then came another swirl out over the groundbait. It seemed that the bream had arrived at last, and here was I, so tired that I could hardly muster the energy to sit over the rods and wait for a proper take.

Once again I climbed into the sleeping bag, having decided to ignore the short bursts from the Optonics and take action only when a steady run was indicated. I dozed, awoken abruptly from time to time by a few sharp bleeps, relaxing again when nothing further happened. I was aware, too, of occasional swirls, far out in the pit.

At some stage of the night I was awoken once again by an Optonic, but this time the chatter continued; I sat bolt upright, and watched the pale shape of the monkey on the crust outfit move jerkily up the stick. When it neared the top, I struck – and missed. Another line bite? It was impossible to say. I baited with another cube of crust, and re-cast.

Shortly after midnight, following a little more fitful sleep interrupted by odd bleeps, the steady tone of an Optonic aroused me, and I looked to see the monkey on the bread outfit climbing smoothly up the stick. I struck at nothing again, but upon retrieving the tackle, I found that the hooklength had parted. Cursing under my breath, I set about tying a new one in the light of a torch. An offer had been missed, almost certainly from a bream; I'd waited so long for the chance to catch one of these fish, that I decided that the opportunity must not be lost for the want of sleep. After re-casting, I sat over the rods, and within minutes the crust was taken again, the monkey ascending the stick smoothly to the accompanying purr of the Optonic. I lifted the rod firmly, and this time felt contact made with a heavy weight which hung deep, unmoving, far out in the pit.

For a few seconds it didn't shift, but gradually it began to yield. It became apparent that the line had sunk amongst weed at the edge of the gravel spit, causing a horrible, rubbing sensation as I tried to guide the fish towards the bank. With direct contact lost, I could feel only a heavy, lifeless weight, and I feared for a while that the hook might emerge with just a clump of weed attached. Then came a big, oily swirl at the end of the spit, and a simultaneous strong thump which caused the rod tip to jag downwards. Across the shallows the fish came, with several more heavy swirls, until it rolled onto its side and in the faint glow of the distant town lights I vaguely distinguished a large, pale shape as it slid across the surface towards the waiting net.

The author's hard-earned 9lb 5oz bream

Moving well back among the grasses, I parted the meshes, switched on the torch and saw the deep, bronze flank of a very large bream glistening in the pale shaft of light. Unable to retrieve the hook, which was lodged well down the throat, I decided to cut the line and attend to the matter during daylight. I found another hook, attached to a short length of line, embedded in the top lip; it was the one which I had lost on the strike, earlier in the night. Lifting the scales, I wondered if the fish might make double figures, but in the torchlight I saw the needle flicker to a halt a little short of that weight, at 9lb 5oz. I secured the bream in a carp sack, which was lowered into the margins before I sat down to sort out the tackle.

There was a diminished amount of bream activity in the swim right through until dawn, betrayed by an occasional swirl or a bleep or two from an Optonic. No more strikable indications occurred, but somehow, it didn't matter; anything else on that night would have been a bonus.

The new day was pleasant to begin with; the surface of the Lagoon was mirror calm, and the sun's warmth soon began to penetrate. During the course of the morning, however, the wind gradually increased in strength, until a heavy swell was pushing down the pit. I added a small common carp to my catch, and pulled out of a tench in the margins, before returning home at noon, still in a state of elation.

The demanding and often very slow fishing provided by extensive, immature pits such as the Lagoon is not every angler's cup of tea. The challenge is a daunting one, but success, when it comes, is all the sweeter for the fact that it has to be earned.

4   The River Nidd

A strange river, the Nidd. In its upper reaches it is much like any other Yorkshire river, running swiftly through a steep-sided, thickly-wooded valley. Pebbly shallows are interspersed with deep pools in which trout dimple on warm summer evenings, modest brownies which nevertheless offer a challenging test for the fly angler. The upper Nidd is not exclusively fly-fishing domain, however; there are grayling for the coarse angler to seek during the hard months, along with pockets of good dace and the occasional bonus chub. But it is downstream of the market town of Knaresborough that the Nidd comes into its own as a coarse fishery. It is unique among Yorkshire rivers in that in its lower reaches it is narrower than further upstream, so much so that in places the bankside willows actually meet across the river. Here, the Nidd is full of character, and there are numerous deep runs and pools, frequently overhung by willows; the trailing branches and probing roots form a haven for chub and barbel, although the barbel in particular tend to be localised and only a handful of swims live up to their promising appearance.

It was through my good friend, Rob Platais, that I was introduced to such a swim; we journeyed there on a warm early summer afternoon, intending to fish until dusk. Rob parked the car on a grassy verge beside an old farm track, we unloaded the tackle and then followed a pathway along the top of the steep banks which border the river. After pursuing the meandering watercourse for a good mile we reached the spot, a place where the river narrows immediately downstream of a wide bend. The far side is congested with willows, and as we stumbled down the sandy bank we disturbed a pair of mallard which were working beneath the overhanging branches; they took to the air with loud splashes before winging swiftly down-river. Rob selected a position directly opposite a small clearing in the far bank growth, and advised me to fish about 10 yards downstream, where there was a similar clearing.

The tactic was to be float-fished maggots, using large balsa floats with the shot bunched well down to get the bait to the bottom quickly. Rob recommended using 4lb line direct to a number 14 hook; I tackled up accordingly, although I had reservations about using such light tackle when barbel were the quarry. A gentle lob was all that was needed to drop the tackle into the far side clearing, and from there it was possible to guide the float downstream, keeping it tight against the trailing willow branches, for it was from this area that bites were expected. Among the branches the current is subdued, but down the middle of the river there is a powerful flow which adds a little to the difficulty of float control. As we tackled up, and during fishing, we continually peppered the swims with loose maggots, throwing them right among the branches. Rob reckoned that heavy loose feeding was essential in order to get the barbel moving, and to this end we took along 3 pints of maggots each.

Rob was first to begin fishing, but he'd had no action by the time I was ready to cast out. He reckoned that it wouldn't be long before one of us was into a fish; apparently the swim had been

The majestic form of a Nidd barbel

82

producing spectacular results of late. While Rob had not as yet managed to break the 6lb barrier, a couple of other friends had grassed several 7-pounders and a couple of 8-pounders. These are fine fish by Yorkshire standards, where generally barbel do not run as large as in some of the southern rivers.

I dropped the float into the clearing and watched it creep gently through the dark, deep water until it was brushing past the trailing branches. Gradually it began to pick up speed as it was caught by the main current, until it was swept out into the open river, away from the area of interest. I retrieved the tackle and repeated the procedure, several times; some adjustment to the setting of the float was necessary, so that the bait was tripping the bottom without catching on obstructions too frequently. Against the far bank willows I found that the depth is around 6 feet. There is a shallow clay ledge on the near side which drops away abruptly about a third of the way across the river; thus the deep water is funnelled beneath the willows to form an obvious holding area for barbel.

On several occasions the float folded under as the hook caught on underwater obstructions. Then, as it ran through the swim again, it disappeared very deliberately, a distinct pluck transmitting through the taut line as the orange tip stabbed into the flow. I swept the rod sideways and connected with something immovable, but very much alive. There was a solid jag as the fish moved for the roots, and a brief struggle ended abruptly when the line fell slack, broken just above the hook. My uneasy feeling about the ability of the tackle to deal with the fish which we were seeking increased. To step up line strength and hook size might result in less bites, but at least it would enable me to hold fish from the growth. I decided to continue with the set-up in use, but to change immediately if another fish was lost.

After tying on a new hook, I re-cast. A few minutes later the float had worked out of the slack and away from the branches, and was sliding down the main flow in the open river. Suddenly it plunged, vanishing into the depths at speed. I struck into something which hung deep in the current for a few seconds before turning and moving forcefully for the willows. Once again the line fell slack; this time the hook had pulled. Before I had finished cursing I heard Rob say something, and I looked round to see his rod well hooped as he too struggled to keep a good fish out of the tangle. Seconds later his rod tip sprang straight: he'd been snapped. I needed no further incentive to make a tackle change. These felt like big fish, and if I hooked another I wanted to be in control right from the start. I therefore opted for 8lb line, fished straight through to a forged, barbless number 10 hook which was baited with four maggots. The barbel didn't appear to be in finicky mood, so I was confident that this relatively crude tackle would still produce takes.

Fifteen minutes passed, during which the stepped-up tackle failed to produce a bite. Once again the orange-tipped float reached the limit of the clearing and began to brush past the first of the trailing branches; as it did so it stabbed under, pausing momentarily beneath the surface before vanishing into the shadow of the depths. A sweeping strike met with something so solid that it could almost have been a willow root, indeed it took a few seconds before I became entirely convinced that I had a fish. Taking full advantage of the strong tackle, I really leaned into it, the rod bent into a wild hoop and the line humming under the strain, despite the fact that there was no breeze to speak of. Yet the barbel was completely unrelenting, a constant, stubborn force thrusting at the roots, sometimes giving a heavy thump or two which caused the rod tip to jag round even further. For a while I even began to doubt that the stepped-up tackle was adequate for the job. At last, however, the fish yielded and moved out into the main flow, still hugging the bottom, still moving with great power, but now I had the upper hand. Beneath the rod tip I piled on the pressure; down below, something gave slowly, until a big, bronze form rolled on the surface. There were just a few more half-hearted lunges as I hustled it into the net.

It was a big fish, of that there was no doubt. As I held it in the net in order to remove the hook, I was amazed by the thickness of its back. The glistening, brassy flanks gave way to a cream-coloured and very solid belly, the orange-tinted fins adding sharp contrast. I lowered it into the margins, still in the net, in order to give it a breather while I prepared the scales and the camera. How big? Certainly a 6, perhaps a 7-pounder, I thought. I don't often catch barbel, and confess that I find it difficult to judge their size. They are very solidly built fish, and often seem to weigh heavier than they look. Rob came down to see the fish; 'It's a monster,' he said, 'it'll go 8lb.' The scales settled at 8lb 2oz. I thought of Rob's quest for a 6-pounder from the swim, and the time he had spent there during the preceding weeks; there is no justice in fishing.

With the fish safely back in the river, I turned my attention to the tackle. The gape of the hook had widened considerably during the fight. The float and shot had slipped approximately 4 feet up the line, presumably as a result of rubbing against the roots as the fish struggled to find sanctuary. The line was quite badly frayed in places, and snapped like cotton when I pulled. All in all, it was a miracle that the fish was landed.

We fished on, but from my point of view anything else would have been a bonus. In any case, the initial burst of activity did not last, and for quite a long period afterwards neither of us had anything to show for our efforts. Early in the evening, I decided to step up the quantity of loose feed which I was introducing, and I was rewarded with a barbel of 5lb 11oz, plus another one lost when the hook pulled free. Poor Rob patiently endured my bubbling excitement, and still had nothing to show for his own efforts; it's not much fun when all the action is falling to someone else's rod, as I know from personal experience. Rob's swim eventually came good, though, and yielded fish of 5lb 11oz and 3½lb.

Dusk approached, the air became perfectly still and the first bats flitted over the shadowy reflections on the river's surface. During the latter part of the evening we experienced numerous sharp dips of the float, some of which we struck, but without success. We attributed these shy bites to chub, and accordingly made no effort to induce more confident takes. When the light levels became so low that we could no longer distinguish our floats, we reluctantly tackled down and followed the path back upstream, chatting contentedly about barbel and barbel fishing.

Needless to say, following such results on my first visit to the swim, I was keen to return. Indeed I did so on several occasions during the following weeks, but I failed to repeat my initial success due largely, I think, to marauding chub. Large numbers of these fish seemed to have taken up residence in the swim, and they fed avidly on maggots, pale flanks sometimes gleaming in the murky water as they rose high to intercept loose feed. Few, if any maggots can have escaped the chub and reached the river bed, and consequently the barbel were simply not aroused.

I caught a few chub, despite the fact that they were obviously wary of the heavy tackle in use; for each fish hooked, there were numerous dips and bobs of the float which were too quick to strike. Since I was, first and foremost, fishing for barbel, I refrained from changing to finer tackle. The chub which I landed were all modest samples, none weighing in excess of 2½lb. I soon came to regard them as a nuisance, and began to consider methods of getting feed down to the barbel, if necessary at the expense of driving the chub away; a friend thinking along the same lines used a bait dropper with moderate success. I did not get round to trying out my own ideas, since my attention was diverted to other waters and I did not fish the Nidd again for the remainder of the summer.

Early the following season, I began to think about those barbel again, and it wasn't long before I returned to the river, this time electing to fish the swim from the upstream position. The water level was an inch or two above normal following recent rain, and the main flow was swirling a little and pushing through faster than usual. The tackle consisted of the same carbon Avon rod which I had used previously, coupled with a fixed-spool reel and 6lb line. At the business end was a 6BB balsa float and a forged, barbless number 12 hook. This set-up was something of a compromise, an attempt to retain a reasonable standard of presentation while providing the strength needed to hold a big barbel out of the roots.

I commenced fishing, running the float as close as possible to the trailing branches, gently guiding it down the swim and easing it free from the occasional protruding twig. For a good half-hour I fished in this fashion, continually casting, trotting and peppering maggots among the willow branches. Now and then the orange tip of the float would dip under, but usually strands of weed trailing from the hook betrayed the fact that it had caught on the bottom. Just once, after an unsuccessful strike, I retrieved a bare hook – no weed and no maggots – and concluded that a fish might have been responsible.

Then came an occasion when I had trotted well down the swim, beyond the downstream clearing; the float had been picked up by the main current and swept into the open river, away from the

Action on the Nidd

branches, when the orange tip vanished again. I swept the rod round hopefully and encountered a heavy, but lifeless resistance, a dead weight which yielded slowly and caused me to wonder if I'd hooked a fish, or just an old branch. It came upstream gradually, still without a tug or a pull of any description, and it was only when I saw that the line had cut across the flow, towards the willows, that I became convinced that I had a fish.

Quite abruptly it came to life, as if it had suddenly realised that something was amiss. With the rod a straining hoop and the line close to breaking point I hung on, as the fish hugged the bottom, repeatedly forging down at the growth. Like the barbel which I had previously hooked in the swim, this one showed quite extra-ordinary strength and staying power, and an ability to find an extra influx of energy just when it seemed that the strain was beginning to tell. It was some minutes before it gave up its drive for the roots, and began to circle in the open river. It came to the top for the first time, a pointed dorsal fin cleaving the surface, but it still wasn't finished and with a heavy splash it ploughed downwards again. A few more swirls and plunges in the turbulent water, and I man-aged to hustle it over the rim of the net.

It wasn't a big fish as barbel go, but it was a fit-looking specimen, thick-shouldered, very solid in the belly and cleanly marked except for a split in the dorsal fin. The scales registered exactly 6lb. After taking a couple of photographs I released it in the shallows, and watched it glide away just a few feet to where the depth drops away abruptly. My last glimpse of the fish was of its broad, thrusting tail as it nose-dived almost vertically down into the murky depths.

I sat down on a grassy patch of bank for a few moments, just to enjoy the mild sunshine, reflect on events so far and regain a little composure. Unperturbed by the recent disturbance, a moorhen was working beneath the willows, half walking, half paddling among the tangled branches at the water's edge, and sending occasional wavelets rippling out into the open river. It gave a cluck in mild alarm as I sent another handful of maggots into the growth, whereupon I picked up the rod and prepared to recommence fishing.

Several casts later the float vanished again, in almost exactly the same place that I had hooked the barbel. This time I wasn't fooled by the lifeless weight which I encountered upon striking. The fish awoke to its predicament sooner than the first one, however, and powered for the roots while still some distance down the swim. I resisted for a while, but suddenly the line fell slack and I found to my dismay that the hook had opened under the strain. After tying a new hook, I moved closer to the area which had produced the bites and ran the float through a few times, thinking that fish might be shoaled tightly. There were no more takes, however, apart from which a mid-river snag, presumably deposited by a winter flood, proved troublesome. After losing a float and opening a hook on it, I decided to return to my original position.

By now, of course, I'd introduced a considerable amount of loose feed, and before long I began to get occasional, sharp bites as fish began to respond to the constant stream of maggots. These offers occurred mostly when the float was tight against the branches in a certain area just a little downstream from the top clearing. Many were too fast to strike, but now and then the orange tip was held down long enough to enable me to set the hook. The culprits were chub, not the modest samples which had plagued me a year previously but big, thick-shouldered fish which pulled for the roots with barbel-like strength. I landed three of them – 4lb, 4lb 1oz and 4lb 5oz – before the remainder of the shoal took fright. After this the swim died, and I eventually moved elsewhere, but managed to add only a solitary, small chub to my catch.

The lower Nidd is a river of interesting potential where big chub are concerned. It has a good head of 4lb-plus fish, and from time to time turns up a truly outsize specimen. A friend has a photograph of a Nidd chub which he caught as a youngster, which pulled his spring balance down to the 7lb limit. The picture gives little guide as to the size of the fish, but I have no reason to doubt his word.

I was back again a couple of weeks later on a morning of strong, gusting winds which made for difficulties in float control, even though I was sheltered to some degree by the steep banks. An hour's fishing from the upstream position produced just a solitary, small barbel which was foulhooked in the pectoral fin. Then, after introducing a handful of loose feed, I thought I saw a movement deep down. I threw in a few more maggots – yes, there it was again, the distinct silver gleam of a flank; the chub had arrived. It wasn't long before they were feeding confidently, with

Marauding chub were often a nuisance on the Nidd

fish sometimes in full view as they cruised through the drifting maggots, picking them off one by one.

Here was a dilemma. My chances of hooking a barbel were diminished by the presence of the chub, so I wanted rid of them, yet it seemed foolish to throw away the chance of catching them, especially with fish in excess of 4 pounds on the cards. I figured that a bait dropper, thrown amongst the shoal a few times, might have the combined effect of driving the chub away, while depositing maggots on the bottom for the barbel to find. First of all, though, I decided to run a single maggot through the swim, still fished on a number 12 hook to 6lb line, and suspended a couple of feet below the float. A long shot, perhaps, but I didn't feel inclined to spend time making refinements to tackle for the sake of catching chub; there would be plenty of opportunity to take them during the winter months, when conditions were unsuitable for barbel. I was mildly surprised, therefore, when the orange tip of the float, after drifting a short distance with the feed, slanted under. Tightening firmly, I resisted the first heavy rush of the hooked fish; several determined efforts to reach the roots followed, then a little wallowing in the open river before the chub came to the net. It weighed 4lb 1oz, a fish marred in appearance by a badly mangled top lip, testimony no doubt to the hamfisted attempts of previous captors to remove barbed hooks.

Within half an hour the unlikely tactic of suspending a maggot on crude tackle had accounted for two more big chub of 4lb 10oz and 4lb 2oz, along with a number of fast dips of the float with which I failed to connect. After this bites dried up, so there was no need to employ the bait dropper; I continued to introduce maggots by hand and reverted to the original tactic of tripping the bait along the bottom. There was no sign of interest from the barbel, however, despite the fact that feed was now getting through.

Eventually, having grown tired of the lack of activity, I moved to fish from the downstream position. With the river back to normal level, the location of the mid-river snag which had troubled me on my previous visit was revealed by a furl on the water's surface. It was now a simple matter to avoid it. After a few possible bites, and a few false alarms caused by the hook catching on obstructions, the float vanished again as it ran through the gap between the trailing branches and the snag. I struck hopefully, and connected. After a brief flurry on the edge of the roots, the fish moved into the open river, plunging repeatedly in the heavy flow, the bronze flank of a good barbel showing fleetingly as it turned close to the surface. There was a moment when everything went solid and I cursed the snag, then there was a sudden movement and the fish was free again. It came to the near bank and wallowed among the long grasses which trailed in the water, then quite abruptly it gave up, turned on its side and seconds later was scooped up in the net.

Although it was a sizeable fish it had a hollow belly which meant that it did not weigh as much as my initial impressions suggested. Nevertheless, at 6lb 14oz I wasn't complaining. While generally in good shape it had a deformed and rather stumpy looking tail, which perhaps accounts for the fact that it did not struggle with the power normally associated with a barbel of such size.

The following hour proved to be quite interesting. Bites, when they came, were restricted to a very precise area of the swim, tight against the branches and several yards downstream of the clearing. There is a certain sub-surface branch in this area which protrudes a little further than the others; its tip, which has accumulated drifting debris, can just be seen when the river is at normal level and colour. It is necessary to guide the float past this branch in order to prevent the tackle from hanging up. Often this results in the float taking a path divergent to the line followed by the branches, but now and then the quirks of the current will cause it to run through just a few inches closer to the growth than usual. On the day in question, it seemed that those few inches were crucial, for it was invariably on the occasions that the bait was a little closer to the willows that the bites occurred. These bites came mostly from barbel; I landed two, weighing 5lb 14oz and 3lb, pulled out of two more and added a bonus chub, a pigeon-chested 4¾-pounder.

It seemed, judging by my results to date, that the barbel had a definite preference for the downstream end of the swim. Perhaps this can be attributed to the shallow clay ledge mentioned previously, which becomes progressively wider along the length of the swim. Thus the deep water is bottlenecked beneath the willows at the downstream end, the type of feature which often seems to attract barbel. I determined, in future, to fish this part of the swim in preference to the upstream area.

Chub proved to be troublesome on my next two visits. On the first occasion I succumbed to the temptation of fishing for them, landing eight which ranged from 2lb to an ounce short of 5lb. The following day, when the chub again began to come up for loose feed, I decided to use a bait dropper in an attempt to drive them away. A friend who had experimented along these lines had introduced large quantities of maggots, ten or a dozen dropper loads, every half hour or so, and had not introduced any feed by hand. While this certainly seemed to deter the chub, I had a feeling that heavy bombardments with a dropper might disturb the barbel too, despite the fact that my friend had caught a few of the latter. I decided to adopt a slightly different approach, introducing a single dropper load every ten minutes or so, and in between feeding maggots by hand. The chub were never completely driven away, but activity did diminish, and I was greatly encouraged by the capture of two modest barbel. Then I hooked another barbel which felt much bigger, a fish of real animal strength; I held it from the roots for a while, but in the end the hook opened under the strain. A little later it happened again with another heavy feeling fish.

In such a snaggy swim I think it has to be accepted that barbel will be lost from time to time, but I felt that the percentage of fish which were escaping was unacceptably high. The weak point in the set-up invariably proved to be the hook. In order to retain a reasonable standard of presentation I felt it necessary to use a fairly small hook, certainly no larger than a number 12; quite simply, there wasn't a model on the market, in the size which I wanted, which was strong enough to do the job. On my next session I determined to experiment with different brands, in an attempt to find the best of the alternatives available.

Up until now my visits to the river had taken place in mid-week, but as my next trip was scheduled for a Sunday, I decided to rise early in order to be sure of securing the swim. I set the alarm for 4am and was fishing by 6am on a grey, cool and breezy summer morning. Feeding was carried out on the same basis as on the previous session, but this time I used a bait dropper right from the start. This seemed to bring about the desired result in that there was little chub activity, save for a solitary fish with a distinctive white mark on the back which for some reason seemed unperturbed by the use of the dropper.

As previously outlined, I had on one occasion found a certain small area of the swim, a short distance below the downstream clearing, to be extremely productive; because of this I began to make occasional casts directly into this area, dropping the tackle beyond the protruding, sunken branch. Precision was vital: a few inches too far, and the tackle was in the branches; a few inches too short, and the advantage over trotting through as normal was lost. At about 7.30am, after making a perfect cast, the float suddenly vanished and I was into my first barbel of the morning, a small one which I estimated at 3lb.

The new brand of hook which I was trying proved to be adequate for this fish, but nevertheless opened up rather too easily for my liking on branches and other snags. I therefore exchanged it for another model which is much used and highly talked of in carp fishing circles; it proved to be the best of the alternatives so far tried. I hit a barbel almost immediately after making the change, the float submerging like a javelin as I tried to ease it past the sunken branch. The fish was solid in the roots before I had a chance to assert pressure, but I was encouraged by the way the hook stood up to the strain of being pulled free.

In mid-morning I again dropped a cast beyond the branch.

After travelling a few feet, the orange tip of the float folded under as if the tackle had caught on a snag, but then it bobbed back up and immediately dipped under again, this time with a sharpness which suggested a bite. Sweeping the rod sideways, I contacted something which quickly yielded and swirled on the surface, where I saw not the suspected chub but a big barbel. It wallowed a little among the outermost branches, but was soon hustled across the flow until it reached the margins, a short distance downstream, where it floundered and splashed on the surface. Taking a few paces along the bank, I reached out with the net and enveloped the fish.

Lowering the net among the thick riverside grasses, I parted the wet meshes to reveal a fine barbel, a thick back of deep chestnut-brown giving way to honey flanks and a solid, cream belly. After recording a weight of 7½lb I lowered the gasping fish into the margins, where it thrust away in a shower of spray. Quite why it gave such a half-hearted struggle remains a mystery.

There was just one more, missed bite before my bait supply ran out and I decided to call it a day. At the time of writing I have not been back since. Having gone some way towards overcoming the difficulties which the swim presents, and having taken another good barbel to add to the 8-pounder which I fluked on my first visit, I turned my attention to different waters and different challenges. No doubt I shall be back at some time in the future, though.

Footnote: Subsequent to the events described here, a hook marketed as the *Super Specialist* has become available. While I have not had the chance to test it on the Nidd barbel, it seems to be appreciably stronger than any other brand, and I feel sure that it will go some way towards solving the problems which I experienced with inadequate hooks.

A magnificent barbel of 8lb 5oz

95

5 Claydon Lake

Claydon middle lake: to those who seek catfish, it's a place which is as revered, if not as exclusive, as is Redmire Pool in carp-fishing circles. And like Redmire, Claydon serves as proof that it is not always necessary to look to large waters when outsize fish are the quarry. The catfish is a species which has always intrigued me, and it was inevitable that sooner or later I would make the long journey to Buckinghamshire in the hope of contacting one of Claydon's giants.

The middle lake is steeped in angling history; many well known anglers have fished there, and written about their exploits. A small number of catfish and zander were introduced in the 1950s, following a netting operation at the Woburn Abbey Lakes. Both species have thrived in the shallow, muddy waters, along with numerous common carp and bream. The once abundant tench and pike have now disappeared, however, although they can still be found in the small, lily-choked upper lake.

I first set eyes on the middle lake on an overcast afternoon in late June, and the first thing that struck me about the place was its size. It is little larger than the average duckpond, and further-more, the water is so heavily coloured that sub-surface visibility must be virtually nil. The margins are thickly reeded, but other-wise weed growth is almost non-existent. The lake is situated in open parkland, and only a handful of trees and bushes are dotted around the banks, most of these being concentrated in the vicinity of the dam.

It quickly became apparent that the lake was heavily populated with carp and bream. Clusters of bubbles, swirls and billowing clouds of black silt were everywhere. This activity was most noticeable in the shallows at the top end of the lake, which were never still, although so heavily coloured was the water that even here, where the depth was mere inches, the fish could not be distinguished except when their bodies broke the surface. I was determined to resist the temptation of trying to catch these fish;

carp and bream I could catch close to home, unlike catfish.

I tackled up in a swim between two hawthorn bushes. On one rod I intended to fish a deadbait for the 'cats', while on the other I would fish a maggot on gossamer tackle, in the hope of picking up a few fingerlings for use as livebaits. The deadbait, a small roach, had deliberately been allowed to decompose for a couple of days, because my information suggested that putrescent deadbaits out-score fresh ones where catfish are concerned. It was fished on a hooklength of 15lb Dacron, which is not only extremely supple, but is also more abrasion resistant than nylon, and is therefore less likely to be bitten through. After casting out the deadbait, I set about tackling up my match rod. The terminal tackle consisted of a black-tipped Canal Crystal float, cocked by three BB shot, and a barbless number 24 hook to a 1lb bottom. I plumbed the depth, and was astonished to find that the swim was barely a foot deep. I was aware that the middle lake was shallow, but until now I hadn't realised just *how* shallow!

A single white maggot was nicked onto the point of the hook, after which I flicked out the tackle and followed up with a handful of loose feed. For a while the float remained motionless, although occasional billowings indicated that a fish or two was moving through the swim. Then the black tip sank slowly into the muddy water. I didn't have chance to strike; as I picked up the rod, a bow-wave cleaved the surface and suddenly the reel handle was spinning as an arrow-fast carp cut through the swim. In a matter of moments the tiny hook lost its hold. So much for livebaits!

I had been under the impression that the middle lake was teeming with bait-sized fish, but it soon became obvious that I wasn't going to catch them in any quantity. I continued to fish with maggots, and subsequently picked up a couple of insipid-looking skimmer bream of about 4oz apiece, rather too large to use as baits. Then I bent into something heavy, which for a moment I thought was another carp; instead of running, however, it simply came to the surface, where it swirled and splashed. It was a better bream, which I estimated at 2lb. After this, the swim went dead, and eventually I packed away the match rod. In its place I used stronger tackle to float-fish a cube of Bacon Grill, which, I hoped, might attract a catfish; if not, I anticipated some lively sport with the carp.

One thing which quickly became apparent is that the Claydon

carp, while they are undoubtedly hungry fish, are not stupid. Not surprising, really, for they have doubtless been subjected to heavy angling pressure over the years. While the Bacon Grill certainly interested them – indeed the float hardly stopped stirring and dipping – there were only a few strikable bites, all of which I missed.

In the evening, several locals arrived to fish for the 'cats'. Most had brought along livebaits, and I found myself wishing that I had been able to obtain a few for my own use. At around 7pm, the breeze, which had at times ruffled the surface of the lake, dropped away. If a catfish was going to be caught, this was surely the time. At 7.30pm, there was a sudden blur of sound as an Optonic burst into life, away down the bank to my right. I saw an angler leap to his feet and move towards his rods, pausing for a moment before picking one up and slamming it hard over his shoulder. It took on a violent curve, and far out in the lake taut line began to cut zig-zags through the surface. I moved closer to watch.

Directly opposite, another angler was holding one of his rods, and at first I thought that the hooked 'cat' must have crossed one of his lines. Seconds later, however, he too struck hard; there was a violent eruption a short distance out in the lake, and I briefly glimpsed a long, sinuous tail as it thrashed the surface. In no time at all, the angler on the far side had hustled his fish into the net wielded by his companion, and it looked big as they struggled to lift it ashore. It was quickly weighed and photographed.

'How big?' someone shouted.

'Twenty-six pounds,' came the reply.

Meanwhile, the angler on my bank was still playing his fish. When it was eventually landed, however, it was no monster, just an exceptionally hard fighter, but still very impressive at 16lb. I returned to my rods, but never felt confident that a 'cat' was going to pick up one of my baits.

Fishing during darkness is not permitted at Claydon, so I spent the night with a relation in Oxford. There was no action to either of my rods during the following day, save for a modest carp and a few missed bites to maggot. I spent the second night fishing a nearby water, again without success, although at dawn I missed a run which was almost certainly from a catfish. This was desperately disappointing, because time was running short and I felt that

I would be lucky to get another chance before I was due to return home.

I spent the following day, which was a Saturday, catching up on lost sleep in Oxford. It was a day of hot, muggy sunshine, and I felt that an evening session on the middle lake could be very worthwhile. I woke up late at 6.30pm, however, which after a 25-mile drive didn't leave very much time for fishing. Nevertheless I decided to make the journey, arriving an hour later to find that many more anglers were present than had been the case on either of the two previous days. Fortunately, most were fishing from the house bank, which left plenty of space on the opposite side of the lake from which to select a pitch.

I set up just one rod, due to the limited amount of time available, and cast out a dead skimmer bream, now very putrid following a day in the hot interior of the car. The bait was so far gone that oil slicks broke the surface when it touched the water, and a rank smell clung to my hands. Subsequent experience has proved that catfish will happily take such baits, but my feeling at the time was that the skimmer was too rotten to be of much use, and after a short while I decided to discard it in favour of Bacon Grill. How I wished I'd capitalised on my chance early that morning.

From all around the lake, bleeps constantly carried through the still, evening air, as anglers adjusted their Optonics. When, at 9pm, another Optonic sounded, it came as something of a surprise to realise that it was my own. I half expected the monkey climber to drop back as a carp mouthed and ejected the bait, but it slid right up the stick and as the line drew tight, I struck hard. Something powerful and heavy began to struggle well out in the lake, moving with violent zig-zagging motions and never running far, although there were one or two short bursts of speed which had line hissing through the water. For a long time the fish remained some distance from the bank, stubbornly resisting the pressure which I applied. Occasionally a vortex or a swirl of turbulence would break the surface, but still I saw nothing; all the time I was wondering if I'd hooked a 'cat', or just a larger than average carp. I took encouragement from the fact that the fight wasn't reminiscent of a carp, in fact it was more in the style of a giant tench. Gradually the fish began to yield, losing ground slowly despite the fact that it still moved with great power. Then a

The 42in landing net looks none too big for this double-figure catfish

broad, mottled back momentarily broke the surface – a catfish, as I'd hoped. With some difficulty I managed to manoeuvre it over the rim of the giant landing net, whereupon I put the rod down and struggled to lift the fish ashore.

It was an average sized specimen by Claydon standards, weighing 12lb 6oz, but to me it was very special, fulfilling a long-standing ambition to catch a catfish. I reeled off a number of photographs before slipping it back into the muddy shallows. I didn't make another cast that evening, having no desire to add to my catch, and the following morning I returned home.

It was at the end of August that I returned to Claydon, this time for six days' fishing in the company of Rob Platais. We pitched a tent at a campsite in Buckingham, which is within easy travelling distance of the lake. After a couple of days fishing a pattern began to emerge relating to the times at which the catfish fed, a pattern which was to be followed for the duration of our stay. The bulk of the action came in the half hour preceding darkness, and often several anglers experienced takes during this period. Otherwise the fishing was very slow, although it seemed that a solitary fish might show at any time of the day.

The three principal baits which we had available were roach deadbaits, swan mussels and Bacon Grill. Conversations with the Claydon regulars suggested that the middle lake 'cats' were mostly caught on squid and small livebaits, however. Both Rob and I felt handicapped, so I decided to give float-fished maggots another try, in the hope of picking up a few fingerlings. It wasn't until I ventured to the tiny upper lake that I managed to catch the bait-sized fish I wanted. Here, I took small roach and rudd without difficulty by fishing clearings among the marginal lilies, although I was hindered by jack pike; they seemed to be every-where, and struck frequently, scattering the fry and leaving clouds of silt billowing through the clear, shallow water.

My efforts to obtain livebaits were repaid during our second evening at the lake; a run came at dusk to a legered roach, and a 'cat' of about 6lb was subsequently landed. While I was well pleased with this fish, it paled in comparison to a specimen which we saw landed on the first evening, a monster catfish of 25½lb, known as 'Mug Jaw'. Easily identified by its protruding lower jaw, it had apparently been caught on numerous occasions since the start of the season, hence the uncomplimentary nickname.

Our third day was bright and warm, with just the lightest of breezes rippling the lake. I spent the first half hour catching livebaits from the upper lake, and when the bucket was brimming with fingerlings, I moved down to join Rob. We fished adjoining swims mid-way along the house bank.

At this point I should explain that an acquaintance from Accrington was also fishing the lake. Early in the afternoon, I glanced towards his pitch, close to the dam, and saw him on his feet, rod well hooped, as he struggled against a good fish. I walked down the bank to watch him land it. As I stood by his side, watching the taut line cutting through the ripple, he explained that already that morning he'd landed 'Mug Jaw'. Imagine his surprise, therefore, when a huge 'cat' with a protruding lower jaw eventually surfaced, and moments later he netted 'Mug Jaw' for the second time that day! Both times the fish had fallen for an eel section bait.

Later in the afternoon, our friend from Accrington departed for home, and kindly gave us his remaining bait, which included half an eel. Rob and I divided it between ourselves, and I cast out a 3-inch-long section on one rod, while continuing to use a livebait on the other.

Evening came, and the breeze abated. As the light began to fade, a heron flapped slowly over the meadow on the opposite side of the lake, uttering a hoarse croak which carried through the still air, before alighting in the highest branches of a distant tree.

A small 'cat' was landed further down the lake, and then, in the gloom at quarter to nine, one of my Optonics chattered into life; the eel section had been taken. I picked up the rod and allowed line to trickle off the spool, as Rob moved stealthily towards the pitch and picked up the landing net. After a suitable period of time, I closed the bale arm and waited until I felt the line drawing tight before hitting the fish hard. There was a heavy and ponderous swirl well across the pool, and in characteristic fashion the fish began to plough stubbornly through the shallow water. It made a long, diagonal run towards a cluster of rushes on the far side, the reel handle revolving erratically as I grudgingly yielded line. Fortunately, the 'cat' turned well short of the reeds, and then lumbered slowly towards the near bank, some distance up the lake from where I stood. I moved towards it, taking in line as I did so, and Rob followed with the net. By now, the fish was wallowing and swirling among the nearside rushes. Under heavy pressure, it came slowly and grudgingly down the margins, towards a gap in the growth where Rob was waiting. A few feet from the net, a large, flat head broke the surface, before the fish powered into the open lake again, although this time it didn't run far. From that brief glimpse, I knew that I had a sizeable fish – about 15lb, I guessed. Pretty soon, it was wallowing in the margins again, and with some difficulty I managed to bully it over the outstretched net. Rob lifted. I slackened, and waited for him to climb up the bank.

'Can you give me a hand?' he asked.

I couldn't understand what the problem was – Rob's a big, strong lad – but I put down the rod and jumped down the bank to where he stood. As we jointly hoisted the fish over the rushes, and

'Mug Jaw', caught at last

I saw its huge bulk doubled up in the bottom of the net, I suddenly realised why Rob had experienced difficulty in lifting it. This 'cat' was more than just good; it was immense, without a doubt the largest fish of my undistinguished angling career. By now, several other anglers had been attracted by the commotion. The net was laid on the grass, scales and a weighing sling were produced and torches flashed shafts of light up and down the glistening hulk of mottled flesh.

'It's "Mug Jaw" again!' somebody said in amazement. I stood back in a trance as the fish was hoisted up in the sling.

'Twenty-five pounds on the dot,' a voice announced. 'Well done, mate.'

The giant 'cat' was placed gently in the landing net again, and Rob held it in the margins while I, still feeling dazed, set up the camera. Then we lifted the fish onto the bank, and I struggled to hold its bulk above the ground while Rob got busy, the dazzling light of the flash gun repeatedly illuminating the surroundings. Moments later I lowered the fish into the margins beyond the reeds. For a second or two it was lost to sight, before there came an enormous swirl, and a huge head rolled across the surface as the 'cat' turned in the shallow water. Then all was still; 'Mug Jaw' was free once more.

As we celebrated in a Buckingham pub later that evening, I suddenly had a terrible feeling that I'd left the lens cap on the camera, and that my fish of a lifetime had been returned without being recorded on film. I felt quite gutted, but as it happened my fears were unfounded and the pictures, when developed, were adequate, if not brilliant.

The fourth day followed a similar pattern to the previous two days, with no action until dusk, when a modest 'cat' of 8lb 5oz fell to a livebait offered on one of my rods.

A problem which we encountered during our days at Claydon concerned the upper lake's roach and rudd, small, frail fish which we had difficulty in keeping alive when we used them as livebaits. Often we would retrieve one after fishing with it for a few hours, to find it lifeless and as stiff as a board. I think that the combination of shallow water and warm weather might have had some influence in their demise, since I have not experienced difficulty in keeping fish baits alive elsewhere. Anyhow, it was clear that rather more robust baits were desirable.

On the following day, we decided to try a method known as 'dipping', which we gathered was a successful means of obtaining bait-sized fish from the middle lake. This involves dragging an outsize landing net through the margins. I was pleasantly surprised to find that it works, and over a period of about ten minutes I was able to gather a selection of small fish including carp, skimmers, roach, gudgeon, lots of tiny zander and even a mini-catfish of 3 inches long! Most of these were returned. I was getting quite carried away and enjoying it almost as much as the proper fishing, when I heard someone shouting from across the field on the far side of the lake. It was the bailiff, and from his gesticulations it was obvious that I was doing something wrong, so

Fingerling zander caught by 'dipping' in the margins at Claydon

I stopped 'dipping' and returned to my pitch.

The weather had taken a turn for the worse, with the skies a sombre grey, threatening rain, and the wind blowing a heavy ripple towards the house bank. My pitch was close to the dam, on the opposite bank to the house so that I could fish with the wind behind me. I erected an umbrella so that I was able to sit in comfort, protected from the breeze and the occasional flurries of rain. One of my rods was baited with a roach livebait, the other with squid which had been given to us by a departing angler the previous evening.

At this stage of the week I'd had more than my share of sport, and I badly wanted to see Rob catch his first catfish. Although he didn't show it, I knew that he was becoming increasingly frustrated, and it only made matters worse for him when fish continued to fall to my rods. But luck is rarely distributed evenly, and when an Optonic chattered into life, surprisingly in mid-afternoon, it was again one of my baits which had been taken. The culprit was a small 'cat' of 7lb 10oz, an unexpected bonus since during the previous few days sport had been restricted almost entirely to the last half hour of daylight. After slipping the fish back into the shallows, I cast out a fresh livebait and sat down again in the shelter of the umbrella.

By now the skies had brightened and the rain had ceased, but the wind still blew relentlessly, and indeed continued to do so throughout the remainder of the afternoon and evening. Even at dusk it didn't moderate, and I wondered if this change in weather conditions might deter the catfish from partaking of their usual late feeding spree. Right at the death, however, there was a sudden blur of sound from one of my Optonics. The squid had been taken, and the line was fairly sizzling away; a few yards vanished from the spool, then I turned over the bale arm and struck. The rod, an old, through-action fibreglass model which I still use because it seems to bring me luck, bowed round, and I could tell by the strenuous, thrusting struggle which followed that the fish was a good one. For a long time it was stubborn and unrelenting, seemingly able to take line at will, and although it never set off on any long runs, it still moved a considerable distance up the lake during the course of the fight. It was hard to follow the movements of the fish in the gloom, as I was unable to see the line, but now and then a heavy swirl in the ripple would betray the whereabouts of the catfish.

I had to shout a couple of times before Rob, who was fishing on the opposite bank, heard me above the wind and came round to assist. He was still fishless, and I felt a little guilty about making him leave his rods at the time when a run was most likely; however, he assured me that he was keen to see my 'cat' landed.

For ten minutes or more the rod remained in a tight curve. The fight was never dramatic, there was simply a heavy feeling of animal strength. Inch by inch, line began to build up on the spool of the reel. During the final stages of the struggle, the fish ploughed into the margins, and the shallow water rocked. Suddenly there was a great swirl directly in front of me, which I can only assume was caused by a carp which had ventured into the area and then taken fright. Eventually the protesting 'cat' was hustled over the rim of the net, and Rob hoisted it onto the bank.

By now, the light levels were so low as to make reading the scales and setting the camera impossible without the aid of a torch. Unfortunately, Rob had lost his, and I'd left mine at the campsite. Only a handful of anglers had fished the lake that day, and of those remaining, only one had a torch, the batteries of

106

which were almost completely run down. However, we managed to extract a faint flicker of light, enough to set the camera and read off a weight of approximately 17½lb.

The following day was our last, and with poor Rob still fishless my only concern was that he should have some action. My prayers seemed to have been answered when in mid-evening he bent into a fish, and I scrambled round to his pitch on the opposite side of the lake in order to help if necessary. When I arrived his rod tip was straight, and the line limp. I tried to console him, but I knew that nothing I could say would make any difference. Fishing can sometimes be a cruel sport. Fate had one more trick to play, however. At quarter to nine, literally minutes before we were due to pack up and set off for home, Rob connected again. This fish remained attached and was subsequently landed. Rob broke his duck in style with a 'cat' of 18lb 10oz.

It was two happy anglers who motored up the M1 that evening.

6 Sallow Pool

Let me begin this account by giving credit where it is due. It was my good friend, Tony Smith, who decided to investigate Sallow Pool, after hearing rumours about its potential. One autumn, he spent a number of days there, fishing for big perch; he caught a few small and medium-sized fish, before finally netting a superb specimen of 3lb 6oz. It was a year after the capture of this fish before he wet a line on the pond again, and in just two further visits, he accounted for two more magnificent perch of 3lb 5oz and 3lb 8oz.

Close examination of the slides which Tony took revealed that the last two fish were, in fact, one and the same. There was a slight scale deformation on the left-hand flank, but the most distinct feature was a dark stripe on the second dorsal fin. His first fish appeared to be a different one.

It didn't take much effort on Tony's part to persuade me to fish the pond. After acquiring the appropriate permit, I made my first visit on a late November day, making for the swim and using the tactics advised by Tony. Not a bite of any description came to my baits, however, and the story was the same on two further sessions during December. I concluded that it was too late in the year for the best of the fishing, and vowed to return at some stage during the following summer.

Although small, covering an area of no more than 2 acres, the pond is unusual in that it is extremely deep; most swims drop away to something in the region of 14–15 feet just a few yards from the bank, making the use of sliding floats necessary even for fishing under the rod end. What sort of depth is to be found in the centre of the pool is anybody's guess; we have never attempted to find out, but it certainly appears that the depth increases steadily in proportion to distance from the bank. There are extensive areas of shallow water in two corners of the pool, where thick beds of crowfoot grow to the surface during the summer months; these shallows are much frequented by coots, moorhens and dabchicks,

Sallow Pool

which undoubtedly find rich pickings as they dive constantly amongst the weed. The crowfoot extends right round the margins of the pond, but despite the crystal clear water, insufficient light penetrates the deep areas to permit the growth of weed.

A small amount of back-filling has taken place along one bank; the hillocks thus created have been colonised by dense thistles, nettles and brambles, making the pool all but inaccessible in this area, although there is a pathway which leads to a solitary, well-trodden swim. It was from this swim, which is adjacent to one of the shallow, weed-choked areas of the pool, that Tony was successful in catching two of his large perch. Looking across the roughly square-shaped pond from here, the far bank is overhung with sallows and hawthorns, interspersed with the odd oak, and again is largely inaccessible; there is a solitary swim tucked amongst the foliage, but to reach it entails pushing through and stooping beneath the dense growth. Thick beds of common reed fill the margins of the left-hand bank, but there are several dilapidated wooden fishing platforms here, which give access to the water. The right-hand bank, on the other hand, is more open, and is understandably the most popular area with the handful of anglers who fish the pool; it is flanked by a small meadow, and again, wooden platforms have been built amongst the sparse rushes in the margins.

Large perch are generally accepted to be very much predatory in their feeding habits, but Tony's attempts to catch them with livebaits had resulted in only a modest fish of 1lb 2oz, and a missed run. The big fish had all fallen to half lobworms, fished on the bottom beneath sliding floats, and had been attracted into the swim by feeding half a dozen chopped lobs at the commencement of fishing, and thereafter, a few maggots and a tiny ball of brown crumb every few minutes. The idea was that the maggots and brown crumb would attract small fry, which in turn would attract the perch. This was the tactic which I planned to use, then, when I returned to the pool on a late August day.

There was a minor setback when I arrived on a grey and rather breezy morning to find an elderly angler occupying the first choice swim, which was of course the one on the back-filled bank. We talked briefly, and I found that he had not, as yet, had a bite. I settled for one of the platforms on the open bank, close to where the only other angler on the pond that morning was fishing. He looked to be a competent fisherman, but reported that all he had caught was a succession of eels up to about 1lb in weight; he had also lost a couple of larger specimens, which had found sanctuary in the thick marginal crowfoot. It wasn't long before he tackled down and left the pond; the elderly angler moved his gear into the newly vacated swim, so I moved mine into the swim which the elderly angler had just vacated!

After positioning the lobworm, which was fished on a number 12 hook to 4lb line, I set about tackling up a second rod. With this I planned to fish a single maggot on a 22 hook to a 1lb hooklength, which would enable me to gauge the response of the small fry to the feed introduced, and also provide a little entertainment while waiting for a perch to appear. Also, of course, the small fish thus caught would make useful livebaits if the lobworms attracted too much attention from eels.

In the event, things didn't work out as expected; by mid-afternoon, there hadn't been a bite to either rod! This was something of a surprise, for in previous seasons Tony had found plenty of action with small roach and perch when he tried maggots. Perhaps the cool, wet weather of the summer in question had some bearing on the apparent lack of small fish.

By now, a little weak sunshine was filtering through the clouds, and although the breeze was still quite stiff, I was nicely sheltered by a tall bank of thistles and was pleasantly warm. It was shortly after 4 o'clock when I noticed the slender black tip of the float on the lobworm rod submerge, very slowly, beneath the surface reflections. Picking up the rod, I paused for a second or two, wondering if the culprit was a big perch, a little perch or just an eel, then a sweeping strike made contact with something stubborn and heavy, which for a moment refused to shift from the bottom. The line began to cut slowly to the right, tangling the second tackle on the way, and I leaned in strongly, aware that the fish was perilously close to the thick crowfoot. It began thrusting heavily and repeatedly at the growth, against all the pressure I dare exert, staying deep down, right beneath the rod end. For a moment it seemed to have found sanctuary, but bending the rod a little more caused the soft weed to part, and the determined plunging recommenced. Once or twice I glimpsed a pale flash deep down, then suddenly the fish gave up and an enormous perch surfaced amid a few fronds of weed. It wallowed and swirled a little as I guided it into the net.

Safely in the meshes, I held it in the margins and dislodged the hook from the corner of its cavernous mouth, then I flung away the weed. On the second dorsal fin I noticed the distinctive black stripe, which identified the fish as the one caught twice previously by Tony. After weighing it at 3½lb and taking photographs, I slipped it back and watched it waddle slowly down the steep marginal shelf, until its outline became faint, and eventually disappeared into the shadow of the depths. I fished on until mid-evening, but there were no more bites.

Naturally, I was keen to return to the pond, but not wishing to catch the same fish again, I decided that my next visit would be spent fishing a different swim. Just a couple of days later I was back, on a bright, warm day with just the lightest of breezes, which left much of the surface flat calm. I walked down the reeded bank, looking at each platform in turn before making up my mind where to fish. Eventually I settled for a swim at the far end of the bank; in order to reach it, I had to push through a shadowy and rather overgrown tunnel through hawthorns. There was just enough room at the water's edge to tackle up, and then by paddling into the shallow water I was able to reach the platform, where I positioned items such as a seat and bait boxes. Leaning over the outermost edge of the platform, I pushed rod rests through a thick carpet of milfoil and into the soft bottom. The water here was the best part of a yard deep, and I was glad of the extending banksticks in which I had invested some years previously. I checked the depth a little further out, in the area which I intended to fish, and found it to be in the region of 14 feet. Then I cast out the two baits, introduced a little feed, and sat back to await events.

On my right, the platform was bordered by rushes, while to the left was an overhanging sallow. A greater threat to my chances of landing a hooked fish, though, came from the soft, dense milfoil which carpeted the bottom up to a point about a rod's length beyond the platform, where the depth shelved away abruptly. However, this was only likely to cause problems if a good fish was hooked on the light tackle in use on the maggot-baited outfit.

In no time at all, the black tip of the float on the lobworm tackle dipped, then ran a short distance across the surface before coming to a halt. Hovering over the rod handle, I waited, praying that the fish would return. In due course the float slowly slipped away, but all thoughts of another 3-pounder were dispelled upon striking, when it quickly became apparent that the fish was of no great consequence. It was soon swung to hand, a plump, dark little perch of about 4oz, which I slipped back off the side of the platform, and watched as it descended slowly into the weed.

A long, biteless period followed, during which I was content to bask in the warm sunshine, or watch lapwings, which sometimes moved over the pool in a large flock from the surrounding fields, tumbling and diving through the air. A smattering of maggots and a small ball of groundbait were introduced to the swim at regular intervals. The groundbait was selected from a commercial range, a red-coloured mix which is supposedly specially formulated for fishing in clear, deep water. I wasn't entirely happy with it, because I found it sank rather quickly, whereas I had been looking for something which hung in a cloud to attract small fry. I remain unconvinced by the extravagant claims made about the many commercially produced groundbaits, baits, ingredients and additives which have appeared on the market in recent years.

Although I continue to experiment with them, I have yet to find anything which significantly improves catches, and I maintain, as I have always done, that there is no substitute for skill.

Early in the afternoon, the maggot float, shotted until it was just a dot on the mirror-calm surface, suddenly vanished. My strike failed to connect, and moments after re-casting, the process was repeated. Then the lobworm float, a few feet to the right, stirred a little before sliding under; this time I felt the fish, momentarily, and then retrieved a chewed worm. Clearly a fish, or a shoal of them, had arrived in the swim and stumbled upon the feed. Whilst in the act of impaling another worm, I glanced up just in time to see the maggot float slip away again. The slender tip of the boron curved as I tightened into the fish, and the worm rod was cast aside, dropped onto the rushes to be attended to later.

When I tried to apply pressure to the hooked fish, it became apparent that it had found a snag, somewhere in the deep water beyond the marginal weed. Moments later there was a sudden movement, and something began to rise grudgingly from the depths, writhing backwards, a familiar struggle which told me that I'd hooked an eel long before I caught the first glimpse of a pale, sinuous outline down below. I had it on the surface for a short while, a specimen of perhaps a little less than a pound in weight, before it twisted once more, the frail hooklength parted, and the fish nose-dived almost vertically down into the weed. Whether this solitary fish was responsible for the brief spate of bites, I don't know, but for several hours afterwards both floats remained motionless.

It was around tea-time that I began to see indications that another fish, or shoal, had arrived in the swim. In the space of perhaps half an hour came three minute dips of the maggot float, tiny bites which could not possibly have been struck, and which left the bait unmarked. This was interesting, because I had experienced similar indications on another water, and the culprits were invariably big roach. I introduced another small ball of groundbait, and a few loose maggots, hoping to hold these hook-shy fish in the swim for long enough to enable me to experiment, in an attempt to persuade one of them to hang on to the bait for a little longer.

The roach in Sallow Pool are something of an enigma. Those that Tony managed to catch were all small ones, yet on both my

previous session and on the day in question, occasional heavy swirls broke the surface, always a good distance from the bank. These swirls were obviously caused by sizeable fish, and it seemed unlikely that perch or eels were the culprits; the only other species residing in the pool, to my knowledge, is roach.

The first tactical change which I tried was to fish well over-depth, so that around 3 feet of line lay on the bottom. I continued to use a number 4 shot, positioned 9 inches from the hook, in order to counter the effect of drag, though this measure was probably unnecessary on the day in question, for water movement was minimal. This was the technique which had proved success-ful in tempting confident bites from the big roach in the afore-mentioned water. However, during the following half hour the float didn't move, despite the fact that I continued to introduce small amounts of feed on a regular basis.

Next, I tried slipping the float back to its original position, so that just a foot of line lay on the bottom, and I removed the stabilising shot. This did the trick. After ten minutes or so, the float dipped slightly and was held flat to the surface, whereupon I tightened gently and encountered the heavy thump of a hooked fish. It was, as suspected, a good roach, which for much of the fight I was able to see as it turned and plunged repeatedly in the clear, sun-illuminated water. Once or twice it came perilously close to reaching the carpet of weed at the edge of the marginal shelf, but in the end it yielded and surfaced on its side, to be enveloped in the meshes of the net moments later.

It was a cleanly marked specimen with a tint of bronze in the scales, and while it was by no means out of condition, there was an indefinable something in its appearance, which suggested that it was, perhaps, a rather old fish. After weighing it at 1lb 6oz, I replaced it in the wet meshes of the net, and then I rushed through the hawthorns in order to release it elsewhere in the pool. By returning it away from the swim, I hoped to avoid disturbing any others which might have been present. But roach are fickle creatures, and sometimes the capture of one of these wary old stillwater specimens is enough to spook the remainder of the shoal. So it was on the day in question, for try as I might, I

A fine stillwater roach

couldn't tempt another bite to maggot.

The evening drifted on, and the light breeze, which had on occasions ruffled parts of the surface, dropped away to nothing. The sinking sun cast a soft, glowing light on the sallows and hawthorns which overhang the east bank. As the light began to fade, swallows and martins were everywhere over the surface of the pool, and an early bat was on the wing, hawking back and forth along the edge of the rushes. It was at about this time when something, a slight movement or sound, perhaps, attracted my attention; suddenly I realised that the lobworm rod was pulling round, the taut line straining down into the water, and the float nowhere to be seen. I made an instinctive grab, and bent into something heavy which ran a few feet and then began to resist stubbornly, hugging the bottom. For a few moments, thoughts of big perch filled my mind, but as the line cut swathes across the surface, it slowly dawned on me that here was an eel – a big one too, by the feel of it. I despise bootlaces as much as the next angler, but big eels are a different matter, and while I rarely set out to catch them, I certainly don't grumble if one picks up my bait.

The struggle was a long one as the eel was gradually worked upwards through the deep water, line gained and then lost again as the fish writhed backwards. Eventually I had it close to the top, but what with the fading light and the heavy billowing movements of the surface, I saw only fleeting glimpses of the pale outline of the eel's underside, or of the snout and gaping mouth which sometimes appeared briefly above the turmoil. Landing the fish presented considerable difficulty, for my 32-inch net wasn't really adequate for the job. Several times the eel was nearly in, but always the tail was outside the rim, and as I tried to lift, the fish slid out backwards. All the time I was thinking about those teeth, hawsering away the 4lb line. Finally, with the fish fairly inert on the surface, I drew its head past the net, until the tail was over the rim, and when I released a little tension from the line, the long, sinuous body folded into the meshes.

With the net in one hand and the rod in the other, I stepped off the platform and splashed ashore to find a safe spot to deal with the fish. The hook had been swallowed, so rather than risk the difficult and potentially harmful job of prodding with a disgorger, I cut the line as close as possible to the eel's mouth. I am quite

A big eel and the bait which was its downfall – a small dead roach

certain that cutting the line is the best course of action with any deep-hooked fish, when two or three dips with a disgorger have failed to retrieve the hook. A barbless hook in particular is likely to be expelled quite quickly, and without any detrimental effect to the fish. I have proved this to my own satisfaction by re-capturing fish which have been treated in this way, whereas I have on more than one occasion witnessed fish fatally injured by well-meaning anglers who were commited to removing the hook.

The eel was a thick, solid and very muscular specimen, which looked as if it might weigh more than my previous best of 2lb 14oz. The scales confirmed this when they stopped at 3lb 9oz. I gave it a breather by retaining it in a carp sack, while I set up my camera with a flash gun. Then I reeled off a few shots, struggling to hold the squirming fish as bright flashes of light pierced the gloom. The eel was then slipped back into the margins, where it swiftly disappeared into the shadows.

Following another, rather nondescript day's fishing at the pond, I came to a decision not to fish there again. The reasons for this were several, not least because to reach the fishery involved a long drive from home. However, when another friend, Jon Wolfe, heard about the perch and expressed an interest in fishing the pond, I ended up making arrangements to meet him there one morning in mid-September. We agreed to see each other on the bank at 8am, but my alarm clock failed to sound and it was 10.30am when I eventually arrived.

Jon had misunderstood my explanation about the location of the 'hot' swim, and was fishing from one of the platforms on the open bank. I was surprised and pleased to learn that he had already caught a big perch, a fish of 3lb 6oz, and even more surprised to hear that it had taken a livebait. After unloading my tackle from the car, I went round to photograph the fish; when Jon pulled his carp sack from the water, I immediately looked at the second dorsal fin, and there was the unmistakable black stripe – the same fish again!

The day was uneventful for me, but not for Jon, who missed two more runs on livebaits. It was inconceivable that the known fish would take baits so soon after being released, so we figured that there must be at least one more perch, of at least reasonable size, lurking in the pool. Jon's experiences also suggested that livebaits were worth a little more attention than I had previously given them.

There was another interesting occurrence in late afternoon, when Jon hooked a big fish on his second rod, which was baited with a lobworm. I watched the struggle for a while from my swim on the back-filled bank, and then decided to walk round for a closer look. By the time I arrived, Jon had lost the fish, and there was a look of disbelief on his face; it was an eel, he told me, which he had lost in the margins, and he reckoned that it was enormous. I pressed him to put a weight on it, which he was reluctant to do, having never previously seen an eel of larger than 2½lb. But eventually he said that he would be surprised if it had weighed less than 4lb.

When we departed that evening, Jon gave me the remainder of his livebaits, about a dozen gudgeon and small roach, and I decided to return to the pool the following day to give them a try. I arrived on a bright, warm morning, when just a light breeze

Jon Wolfe displays the oft-caught Sallow Pool perch, which on this occasion weighed 3lb 6oz

rippled the surface, and I elected to fish from the open bank. One rod was tackled up to float-paternoster a live gudgeon, the other to leger a gudgeon head section, the latter aimed at attracting a big eel.

During the course of the day, there was one take to each rod. The first came to the livebait, which had been working vigorously, causing the float to bob under on occasions. Early in the afternoon it submerged again, but this time it stayed under, and line began to draw slowly away. At this stage I should explain that when I tied the hook to the line, I hadn't been entirely satisfied with the knot, but I had decided to make do. I struck, bumped something, and retrieved the tackle minus hook.

The take to the deadbait was unnoticed until I tried to wind in for a bait check in mid-afternoon, when I thought for a moment that the tackle was snagged. But the 'snag' pulled back, and a short while later a good eel, which I estimated at 3lb, was writhing on the surface. As I reached round for my giant-sized 42-inch landing net, brought along for just such a fish, the rod tip suddenly sprung straight. Close inspection revealed that the Dacron hooklength had frayed on the eel's teeth. A Dacron hooklength had seemed like a good idea, since this line is widely used to resist the abrasive teeth of catfish. In future I shall revert to nylon for my eel fishing; I have never been happy using wire traces for this species.

With what remained of the livebaits, I returned to the pool again two days later. Having woken that morning with a stinking cold, it was only the mild sunshine and the still air that persuaded me to fish at all. I selected the same swim on the open bank, and on this occasion fished a roach livebait on one rod, and a lobworm on the other. Incidentally, for those like myself who prefer to use barbless hooks, here is a useful tip for preventing livebaits from escaping; it's an idea which I certainly don't claim was my own, but I do not recall having previously seen it mentioned in writing. Simply cut a small piece, about a centimetre long, from an elastic band, push the point of the hook into one end, and slip the elastic round to the shank. Lip hook the livebait, then push the other end of the elastic over the point, effectively locking the bait onto the hook, although of course it can easily be removed when desired. Don't forget to push the elastic round far enough to leave the point and a little of the bend of the hook exposed.

Things were rather slow on the day in question. Indeed, by 4pm there had been no action, save for a couple of abortive takes on lobworm, undoubtedly eels but not necessarily big ones. The roach livebait seemed to have exhausted itself; the frantic noddings and bobbings of the float had stopped, and it had been all but motionless for an hour or more. So when it disappeared, quite suddenly, I knew at once that there was a perch around. Picking up the rod, I waited a few seconds, until the limp line between the tip and the surface picked up and began to draw slowly away. A sweeping strike saw the rod take on a good curve and kick hard, as a sizeable fish began to struggle. It didn't move far, but bored heavily along the edge of the marginal weed growth; in fact, so restricted was its movement that for a while I thought it might be an eel. Before long, though, the unmistakable form of a good perch was glimpsed as it plunged determinedly in the clear water, and shortly afterwards it swirled heavily on the surface, almost beaten. Even before it reached the net, though, I could see the black stripe on the second dorsal, and the scale deformation on the flank. I didn't bother to photograph the fish, but quickly checked the weight which, according to my scales, was 3½lb again. Moments later the perch was back in the margins, and I watched it waddle slowly away over the thick weed growth. The remainder of the day passed without event.

With every capture of the fish it seemed less likely that another big perch inhabited the pool; on the other hand, Jon's two missed runs suggested otherwise. While the fish responsible for those takes might not have been outsize specimens, I figured that only a perch of reasonable proportions was likely to tackle a livebait in the 3-inch range, and on this basis I determined to visit the pond again the following weekend. I managed to obtain a handful of bait-sized roach in advance, and although they were slightly larger than I would ideally have liked, I decided to make do.

Heavy mist hung over the pool when I arrived in mid-morning, restricting visibility to a few yards. A platform mid-way along the reedy bank was selected, and plumbing revealed that the depth here was rather less than in the other swims which I had fished. I found that a cast of around 15 yards would put the bait in 10 feet of water. As usual I used two rods, offering a livebait on the usual float-paternoster rig with one, while with the other I presented a caster on fine tackle beneath a sliding float. I fed loose casters and small balls of brown crumb on a regular basis, hoping that my caster-baited outfit might tempt one of the pond's elusive large roach.

A heavy dew was still clinging to the rushes which bordered the platform, to the surrounding undergrowth and to a multitude of cobwebs amongst the foliage, the latter quite stark in outline, silver in appearance due to the accumulated drops of moisture. My jeans were quite damp after having pushed through the thick growth, but I knew that it wouldn't be long before the warm early autumn sunshine burnt away the mist and dew, and dried my clothing. Meanwhile, visibility was still very restricted; before me lay a glassy calm sheet of water which gradually merged into greyness. The floats stood out starkly, the one which supported the roach nodding occasionally to the workings of the bait. The only sounds to break the stillness were the occasional, sharp squawks of waterhens, and once or twice an audible swirl as one of those mystery fish broke the surface, out in the mist.

Presently a light, but cool breeze began to ripple the surface, and it wasn't long before it became apparent that the mist was lifting. To begin with, the pale, almost imperceptible silhouettes of the far bank trees became evident in the murk. By the minute their outlines became more distinct, until within half an hour all traces of mist had gone, and I found myself basking in warm sunshine. The gentle breeze continued to blow; although it wasn't strong, it was enough to cause slight discomfort, which it seemed pointless to endure when by making the short move to the opposite side, I could find shelter and flat calm water. Gathering together my tackle, I stepped off the platform and pushed through the growth; already the dew was gone, and the cobwebs were invisible among the grasses.

Arriving on the open bank, I headed for the final platform, tight against a large, overhanging sallow, which marked the limit of the heavily overgrown east side of the pool. Depositing the tackle, I observed the water and watched with interest the dimples caused by a flotilla of tiny fry, which were moving beneath the surface, just a few yards out. Sometimes I'd see a glint of silver as one of these minute fish turned, flank catching the sun. More interesting, every now and then as they drifted around in a confined area, they would suddenly panic and scatter across the surface. It looked very much as if something was striking from below; as if to confirm this, half a dozen fry sprayed out of the water again, and there was a humping and billowing below them.

Pulling another rod from the holdall, I feverishly threaded line through the eyes and tied a small, silver and red spinner to the business end. Ten minutes were spent working it through the area: fast, slow, deep, shallow, pauses, spurts, I tried everything, but there was no response. The fry continued to drift aimlessly, still scattering from time to time. Putting the spinning rod aside, I looked again to the livebait outfit, adjusting the float for the deeper water and re-hooking the roach. Out it went, shattering the calmness as it splashed into the water; the line, I noted, was draped across a large raft of floating weed – crowfoot, beginning to die back with the onset of autumn. I chose not to re-cast for fear of creating further disturbance.

Minutes later, while attending to other matters, I glanced towards the tackle, just in time to see the limp line tighten suddenly, and the rod jolt in the rests. I made a grab, struck firmly, and the carbon curved to the heavy thrusting of a good fish. A short struggle of much power, but restricted movement followed, until there came the now familiar, but nevertheless impressive sight of a sizeable perch breaking the surface in a heavy swirl, before plunging forcefully for the weed again. Heaved upwards, it swirled once more, and it was then that I glimpsed the not altogether unexpected, but nonetheless disappointing black stripe on the second dorsal fin. I didn't bother to weigh the fish on this occasion; instead I returned it immediately, rather than add to any stress which it may have suffered as a result of being caught and handled so frequently.

One interesting thing which came to light as a result of this latest capture was the discovery of a rusting hook lodged in the roof of the fish's mouth. I am almost sure it was the hook which I lost two sessions previously, when the knot failed on the strike. Obviously, I had overlooked it on the previous occasion that I caught the fish.

So that made six times that the perch had been caught by friends or myself, and one occasion when it had been lost; how much longer do you continue fishing in such circumstances? But for the missed runs experienced by Jon, I would have been disinclined to visit Sallow Pool again, other than to fish for eels or roach. Jon was in favour of having another try for the perch, though, so I agreed to accompany him on an early October day.

Weather conditions were rather wild on this occasion; grey, sombre skies threatened rain, and there was a strong, gusting southerly wind. Jon was in the process of tackling up when I arrived, shortly after 8am. Again, he had chosen a swim on the open bank; I decided to push through the sallows and hawthorns to reach the only swim on the overgrown east bank. Here, the bushes afforded a little shelter from the wind, and while the water's surface in the immediate vicinity was by no means calm, it lacked the 'chop' which was evident in more exposed areas of the pool. The swim was unkempt in appearance, and had probably been fished little, if at all, during the summer. There was a clearing amongst the undergrowth, encroached by sprigs of rose hip, which was just large enough to accommodate my tackle. Between the rushes which sprouted in the margins was an opening where several rotting wooden stakes, which had once supported a platform, protruded from the water. Despite the overgrown nature of the swim, it offered a cosy position from which to fish, nestling amongst hawthorn, elder and brambles, and another plus was that this area of the pond had not previously produced the known perch.

One problem which was immediately evident was the amount of crowfoot which had died and was drifting in the surface layers; it had accumulated in some quantity in the margins, forming a carpet up to a distance of about 6 feet from the bank. To overcome this I extended the handle of my landing net to maximum length, so that I could reach over the weed to land a fish, if necessary. As usual, I chose to use two rods, float-paternostering a gudgeon livebait on one, and float-fishing a single caster to a 22 hook and a 1lb hooklength on the other.

Soon after I commenced to fish, the wind veered round a little to blow from a south-westerly direction; this made fishing less comfortable, with a heavy ripple rolling across the swim from left to right, and drifting rafts of weed became increasingly evident, sometimes fouling the lines and dragging the floats under. Then heavy rain came sweeping across the pool, the wind tending to drive it beneath my umbrella, so I was glad that it proved to be nothing more than a shower, which blew over quite quickly. Soon afterwards, Jon pushed through the sodden undergrowth to tell me that he had just missed a good run on a livebait.

At about 10am came what appeared to be a bite to caster, when the black-tipped float vanished suddenly into the waves; my strike seemed, for a moment, to have made contact, but it quickly became apparent that the resistance against which I was bending the rod was lifeless – a snag. Unable to free the tackle, I pulled for a break. While tying a new hooklength, I noticed, but ignored the disappearance of the livebait float; what with the waves, the drifting weed and the energetic workings of the bait, which combined to cause the float to submerge frequently, I didn't suspect a take. Moments later, though, I saw the taut line straining, and the rod tip pulling round; I reacted instantly and struck hard.

The fish hung deep in the wind-swept water for a while, moving little, and then cut slowly towards the bank. With a series of heavy, downward thrusts, it forged along the edge of the accumulated weed, until seemingly it tired and began to yield. The deep flank of a sizeable perch broke the surface with a swirl, which left a calm patch in the ripple. Suddenly the fish plunged, the speed and strength of its dive taking me by surprise and forcing me to backwind. It then resumed its dogged, deep-down struggle, at one stage making a heavy run to the left, which took a few more turns of line off the reel. In the end, though, I had it wallowing among the waves, just beyond the floating weed, and at full stretch I managed to draw it over the net.

Parting the meshes, I saw the familiar black stripe on the second dorsal fin. I slipped the fish back without weighing or photographing, and pushed through the bushes to see Jon. We concluded that his missed run, earlier in the day, might well have come from the same fish as it patrolled the margins of the pond.

Thereafter, there was no action to either rod until late afternoon, by which time the wind had dropped considerably and the grey clouds had been replaced by hazy sunshine. A handful of late swallows and martins were skimming the rippled surface; very soon they would be gone, testimony to the passing of another summer. Meanwhile, on several occasions I thought I had seen delicate, almost imperceptible movements of the caster float. Then the black tip, riding the ripple, gave a distinct double dip; my strike picked up a large amount of slack line and made no impact, but nevertheless on tightening I felt the thump of a hooked fish. The struggle which followed was unspectacular, a

An immaculate Sallow Pool roach

sullen weight yielding grudgingly from the depths until the dark back and dorsal fin of a good roach cleaved the ripple, glistening in the weak sunshine. A few more swirls and plunges and it was drawn towards the extended net.

Bronze tinged and weighing 1lb 6oz, it was a carbon copy of the roach which I caught in August, indeed it might have been the same fish. There were no more bites to either of my rods during the remainder of the day.

At the time of writing, I have not returned to the pond since that October day; no doubt I shall do in the future, though probably to fish for eels or roach rather than perch. It remains a mystery as to whether any large perch, other than the known fish, inhabit the pool. Just to add a little more intrigue, in the middle of that October afternoon, Jon failed to connect with another run to a livebait.

7 Oak Beck

The potential of a tiny north-country beck first came to my notice when a friend, Steve Rhodes, fished it and took several nice grayling, the best a beauty of 1lb 14oz. A grayling of such size is an exceptional specimen, especially to someone like myself who is accustomed to catching fish which usually weigh ounces, and rarely more than a pound, from rivers such as the Wharfe and Nidd. Furthermore, it seemed that the beck might offer some interesting pike fishing; Steve had spotted several jacks, and on one occasion a small grayling had been snatched from his hook while being played. In such narrow confines, I felt that even a modest pike would provide plenty of excitement.

The beck is an insignificant-looking watercourse, rush-fringed, swift-flowing and for much of its length almost narrow enough to jump across. Nowhere in the half mile or so to which I have access does the depth exceed 3 feet, although because the stream permanently carries a touch of colour, the bottom and often the fish remain hidden in the deeper areas. Even in the depths of winter there are lush beds of streamer weed and starwort, which undoubtedly harbour a rich variety of insect life upon which the fish thrive.

On my first visit, the beck carried the grey tinge of melted snow and I failed to tempt a bite, but at least I was able to familiarise myself with some likely looking swims in preparation for my return, which was on a bright February morning. I parked the car among farm outbuildings and followed a mud track through the fields, where iced puddles filled the ruts cut by tractor wheels. Traces of snow were still in evidence beneath the hedgerows, following a light fall some days earlier. Arriving at the beck, I headed straight for a swim of which I had made a mental note on my first visit, a sharp bend where the current undercuts the far bank, and the depth drops away beneath an overhanging stump upon which drifting weed collects. Where the beck straightens below the stump, it continues to run deep for several yards. The

Small stream fishing in summer

far bank is thickly wooded just here, and it is quite common during the winter months to see long-tailed tits flitting through the bare sallow branches, or to hear the drumming of a woodpecker from deeper in the woods.

I tackled up with a match rod and a centrepin reel. A small stick float was selected and shotted so that just a tiny dot of the yellow tip hung in the surface film. Bait was a single white maggot on a barbless number 18 hook, and before commencing to fish I tossed in a few loose maggots at the head of the pool, so that they would sweep down the flow to reach the bottom in the vicinity of the overhang.

The first few casts brought no response, although the float did fold under on a few occasions when the hook caught in debris on the bottom. It wasn't until I allowed the float to run down below the overhang that I had my first bite, but I only succeeded in pricking the fish. A few casts later came another offer in the same area, and this time when I tightened I felt the lively struggle of a grayling in the heavy flow. From my brief glimpses of the fish as it plunged in the current I knew that it wasn't a big one – half a pound, perhaps – but it fought doggedly to hold its position at the tail of the pool. Soon, however, it had tired sufficiently to be guided, still protesting, to where I waited, and as it plunged half heartedly beneath the rod tip I reached down for the landing net. As I did so there was a sudden violent swirl, and I looked up in time to see a big pike, which I estimated at around 12lb, move away in the direction of the stump. It had, of course, engulfed the grayling.

After a few moments I tightened gently, but I couldn't do much with the fish on a 2lb hooklength. It just hung deep in the flow, somewhere beneath the overhang, probably unaware that any-thing was amiss. The float remained visible not far beneath the surface, occasionally cutting sideways a little as the pike shifted position in the current. After perhaps thirty seconds the rod tip sprang straight, the hooklength having been bitten through.

I immediately retreated to set up a pike rod, feverishly threading 11lb line through the eyes, before attaching a float and a braided wire trace. The hook was a number 8 double, and I flattened the barb on the large hook before burying the small one in the head of a still half-frozen sprat.

Meanwhile the skies had taken on a sombre grey hue, and as a flurry of snowflakes began to flutter down, I lobbed in the bait at the head of the pool and watched the orange-topped float wobble erratically down the flow. When it drew level with the stump I gave several sharp twitches, then held back on a tight line, causing the sprat to dart upwards through the murky water before slowly fluttering down towards the bottom again. The tackle gradually swept across the current towards the shallows on the inside of the bend. Suddenly, close behind the bait, a mottled green form loomed out of the depths. With the air still heavy with falling snow I watched, intrigued, as the fish held position in the shallow water, its shovel face mere inches from where the sprat lay on the bottom. I twitched the bait again; it shimmered silver before settling, and the pike edged closer, but still didn't take. Gradually the big fish drifted back towards the depths, until it was no more than a shadow in the grey tinged water, and then it melted away completely. I ran the sprat through the swim several more times, but the pike didn't want to know, so rather than risk disturbing it, I decided on a different course of action.

Picking up the match rod, I tied on a new hook and nicked a maggot onto the point. I ran the float past the overhang a few times, although in truth I thought that the recent disturbance would render it necessary to move to another swim in order to catch a bait sized fish. After a few casts, though, the yellow tip dipped, and I whisked out a 2oz dace before the pike had chance to grab it. A God-send! I nicked the hook into its top lip, lowered it into the current and watched as the float swept downstream. About a yard before it reached the overhang I vaguely saw the dace rising towards the surface, before suddenly the pike came rushing from the depths and took with a violent swirl. The float plunged, arrowing downstream before veering round to hang beneath the stump. I struck hard, felt the solid weight of the fish for a fleeting moment and saw the flash of green flank in the murky water before the hook sprang free. I cursed under my breath. The pike had felt the hook only briefly, however, and I felt that it might still be tempted, providing that I could obtain another livebait.

A frantic half hour in pursuit of a bait finally came to an end when the float dipped at the tail of a long glide, about a hundred yards upstream from the pike swim. A tiny grayling of 4 inches long came flipping to the bank, whereupon I grabbed my tackle and hurried back downstream. After nicking the hook into the grayling's top lip, I lowered it into the shallows and gave it a few moments to recover strength, before lobbing it into the flow. Close to the overhang I held back, and the float gradually weaved across the current towards the inside of the bend. Suddenly the pike was there, evilly green in the shallow water. I tried to entice it by drawing the tackle upstream, but the small grayling, darting in the current, aroused no response. When the bait was well upstream I lifted it out, lobbed it back into the flow and allowed it to swing round in front of the pike, which was still visible in the shallows. For a few seconds there was no reaction, then suddenly the big fish lunged forward. I saw the white inside of its jaws, a cloud of disturbed silt swept downstream and the pike vanished into the deep water, leaving the pool rocking. The float remained visible, hanging motionless beneath the surface, close to where the weed-festooned stump protruded from the far bank.

I wound a few turns of line onto the reel, and then bent into the fish. For a few seconds it just hung solidly beneath the overhang, then it surged down to the tail of the pool and bored heavily in the deep water. Back up to the stump, and the pike's pale flank gleamed in the murky water as it flared its gills and shook its head in an effort to throw the hook. It didn't succeed, but at that moment the half-pound grayling which I'd lost earlier in the day popped up to the surface and floated away downstream. The struggle continued, stubborn and unspectacular, with the fish seemingly loath to venture far from the scant cover of the overhang. Once, it came meekly into the shallows, and for a moment I had it resting on the rim of my inadequate 32-inch landing net, but as I struggled to manoeuvre the fish in the strong flow, it thrust away again with a heavy swirl. Now I knew that it was larger than I had initially estimated, indeed I thought it might weigh as much as 15 or 16lb. Next it moved upstream with several short, but powerful surges, but there was no sanctuary up there and eventually it came wallowing down towards the shallows again, only to thrust away once more when it saw the net. In the end, by positioning the net downstream of the pike, I managed to guide it head first through the frame. Half way in the fish gave another powerful thrust, but only succeeded in burying itself completely in the meshes.

As I struggled to lift the pike up the bank, and saw its primrose-flecked bulk doubled up in the net, I realised just how far out my initial estimate of its size had been. It was not only longer than it had appeared in the water, but it was a deep fish too, probably carrying spawn. The scales didn't settle until they reached the figure of 23¼lb. Whether the fish was a resident of the beck or had run up from the main river to spawn, I don't know. I never saw it again, but then the beck's pike seem to be very nomadic and rarely remain in the same swim for long.

Following such drama it was some time before I recovered composure; my concentration suffered, and I failed to tempt a bite during the remainder of the day. A week later I returned, this time determined to come to terms with the beck's grayling.

It was a still, damp morning, the air thick with mist and the bankside vegetation heavy with moisture. I headed for the swim which had produced all the excitement on my previous visit, and began to tackle up. The crackle of a bonfire carried through the still air, but it was some time before the mist lifted sufficiently to enable me to make out the flicker of flames and the distant figure of a farm hand, who was working across the field. Otherwise there were few sounds to break the silence; just the occasional rustlings of a blackbird among the carpet of dead leaves beneath the dripping far bank trees, or the raucous cawings of a passing flock of rooks.

This time I tackled up with a 22 hook to a 1lb bottom, reasoning that the beck contains few snags and therefore fine tackle could only improve my chances. A few drops of cream flavouring were added to the maggots, partly because they were a little sweaty and I wanted to hide the unpleasant odour; also, I'd had encouraging results in the past after treating maggots in this way, although of course it would be naive to attribute my success directly to the flavouring.

Running the float down past the overhang, bites soon began to come, sometimes just sharp, unstrikable dips while on other occasions the float stabbed under deliberately. Several small dace and grayling came splashing to the bank. Once I purposely spent longer than usual playing a dace, just to see if there was a pike about, but nothing happened, so I lifted out the fish and released it in the margins. Several casts later the float folded under, tight against the trailing weed which hung to the stump, and this time when I tightened it was quickly apparent that a better fish was hooked. After a determined struggle in the heavy flow, a fair grayling swirled on the surface, briefly exposing a large, crimson-tinted dorsal fin. It was netted moments later, and I estimated its weight at ¾lb.

The mist was lifting slowly, although the sky remained grey and the sun never broke through. In the uppermost branches of a far bank tree, gaunt and thick with ivy, a jay alighted, only to flit away into the woods when it spotted me moments later. By now, bites had all but dried up; indeed I was contemplating a move downstream when the float submerged, just a yard or so below the overhang. When I tightened, there was a solid thump and a flash of lilac deep down in the murky water, which told me I was into a good grayling. The fight was rather strange, the fish for much of the time just hanging in the flow, now and then boring away and once clearing the surface in a spectacular trout-like leap beneath the far bank grasses. I held on carefully, biding my time until the grayling was tired enough to be guided over the rim of the net; a

A bedraggled author with his 23¼lb pike

typical beck fish, plump, richly scattered with dark spots and subtly tinged with burgundy and mauve. It weighed 1lb 9oz.

Shortly afterwards I decided to move, first to a long, shallow glide which produced several reasonable fish, and then to the downstream limit of the stretch, where there is a fast, swirling run of around 2 feet deep which cuts through thick beds of streamer weed. A dyke enters the beck at this point, although its flow is negligible and doesn't affect the nature of the swim; indeed on the day in question the dyke was still covered in ice, following cold weather some days earlier.

It was here that I was once lucky enough to see a stoat. Advance warning of its approach came when a moorhen was flushed from the bankside foliage, some distance downstream, to alight in the water clucking in alarm. Moments later the sleek animal appeared from behind a cluster of stunted sallows, bouncing over the thick grasses. It spotted me and sat bolt upright, nose twitching as it watched curiously from across the beck. Then it continued on its way, a little more hastily I fancied, soon to be lost to sight amongst the undergrowth.

A few loose maggots were dropped in at the head of the run, and I followed up with the tackle. The float stabbed into the flow as it ran close past the streamer weed on just the second cast. On striking I half expected to find the hook caught in the weed, but I was pleasantly surprised when the rod bucked as a lively fish plunged in the current. It was coaxed upstream quite easily, but then it resisted stubbornly beneath the rod tip, forging and thrusting against the swirling water. Now and then I caught a glimpse of the fish, a shadow in the turbulence, and I knew that I had another better than average grayling. Finally it rolled into the net, a dark-coloured specimen bearing a well-healed scar close to the tail, possibly the result of an encounter with a pike. Although I felt it would weigh rather more than the big fish I had taken earlier in the day, I was proved wrong; the scales settled at an identical weight of 1lb 9oz.

After returning the grayling a short distance upstream, supporting it in the shallows until it revived, I returned to the swim and missed another bite almost at once, retrieving a well-sucked maggot. By now it was late afternoon, the mist was descending again and the light was beginning to go. I strained my eyes to see the float, a tiny dot of yellow well down the swim; it vanished, but a sweeping strike met only slight resistance and I began to crank a small dace upstream. It had travelled just a few feet when it began to flip and splash on the surface. Suddenly there was a bow-wave, then the rod jerked in my hands and there was a heavy swirl which sent water lapping against the banks. I paused, then tightened and momentarily felt the solid weight of the pike, before the rod tip sprang straight as the line was bitten through.

After tying on a new hook and running the float through the swim a few times, another dace was hooked, and whisked out of the swim as quickly as possible, before the pike had a chance to attack. The fish was retained in a bait box, filled with water, while I set up a livebait rig. However, I decided against attempting to catch the pike until I was sure that the swim held no more grayling which might be willing to feed. Twenty further minutes spent trotting maggots produced only a handful of dace, though, so with a gloomy winter evening rapidly drawing in, I picked up the pike rod.

The dace kicked as I lowered it into the current, and the orange-topped float nodded erratically as it worked down the swim. The tackle had to be retrieved on a couple of occasions when the bait buried in streamer weed, so I decided to lob it some distance down the swim, to the area in which the pike had shown. It landed with a heavy splash, and as the ripples subsided I watched intently, expecting the take to come at any second. After a few moments there was a slight humping on the surface, as if something down below had moved suddenly. The float remained unmoved. Very gently, I tightened and began to draw the tackle upstream, because I suspected that the pike had taken the bait without moving away and signalling a run. It hadn't. I retrieved the tackle and lobbed it back down the swim again. This time the dace had hardly settled when there was a sudden violent swirl, and the float was gone.

After a pause of a few seconds, I wound down to the fish and leaned into it. For a while it held position well down the swim, a stubborn and unrelenting weight, but suddenly it yielded and allowed itself to be guided upstream quite easily. It surfaced beneath the rod tip and hung in the flow, in full view, for a moment or two; a sleek pike which I estimated at 5lb. With a powerful thrust of the tail and a heavy splash the fish plunged away again, forging into the flow and making several dives into the streamer weed, without managing to find sanctuary. Then, as it wallowed gently in the margins, I engulfed it in the meshes of the landing net, whereupon it came to life again and thrashed wildly as I lifted. I took the net to the top of the bank and laid it among the matted grasses, intending to unhook the pike, but the hook had already fallen from its jaws. As with the big pike taken a week earlier, this one had looked deceptively small in the water; in fact it weighed 10lb 6oz.

By now the mist and the fading light had combined to bring the day's fishing to a close, so after releasing the pike at the mouth of the dyke, I tackled down and followed the gloomy track back through the fields.

With the coarse-fishing season rapidly drawing to an end, I was keen to spend at least one of the remaining days on the beck. On the final Saturday, Tony Smith and I decided to make an early start, choosing to fish a different stretch this time, close to the beck's confluence with a small river. We arrived shortly after first light on a grey and cold morning, but we were disappointed with what we found. The lower reaches of the beck had apparently suffered at the hands of the Water Authority, and we soon lost confidence in the straight, featureless and very fast-flowing

Snow scene on the Oak Beck

waterway. In mid-morning, with just a solitary, tiny grayling to show for our efforts, we decided to cut our losses and head upstream to the tried and tested stretch.

As usual, I opted to begin fishing in the swim which had produced the big pike, while Tony wandered off upstream. Several grayling fell to my rod, the largest a little over the pound, but with each fish landed bites became less frequent as a result of the disturbance. Ten or fifteen minutes had passed without a bite when the float folded under, as if the hook had caught on the bottom, after I had allowed the tackle to run right through to the tail of the swim. When I tightened, though, there was a heavy movement in the flow, and the fleeting, pale gleam of the flank of a good fish in the grey-tinged water. The fight was different, yet familiar, an altogether less frantic struggle than that given by most grayling, with a great deal of hanging in the current, the fish combining its weight with the flow in a way which made it difficult to control on light tackle. It was eventually subdued and found to weigh 1lb 9oz, and though I can't be sure, I suspect, because of the peculiar fight, that it was the same fish which I caught from the swim on my previous visit.

After returning the grayling I wandered downstream until I arrived at a swim very similar in nature to the one I'd just vacated. Here, the beck curves sharply and water runs deep beneath the far bank. A knot of stumps protrudes over the surface, accumulating drifting weed to form a raft which looks an obvious attraction for fish. Despite the promising appearance of the swim, which incidentally is one of the deepest on the stretch at a good 3 feet, it had failed to produce a bite on any of my previous visits. Nevertheless I wasn't discouraged from fishing there, because I suspect that many swims on the beck have transient fish populations.

I moved stealthily towards the pool, fishing from a position well upstream and trotting down towards the raft. However, it wasn't long before the hook became firmly stuck in an underwater obstruction, and in order to free it I had to move down the bank, thus undoing all my careful approach work. I ended up standing directly opposite the raft, and although I suspected that any fish present would have been spooked, I decided to try a few more casts before moving on.

After running the float through several times, it submerged, tight against the raft. There was a sharpness in the way it disappeared which suggested a bite, but upon tightening, I thought initially that the hook had caught on the bottom again. For a few seconds I felt just a solid weight, before something began to yield slowly, then suddenly the 'snag' came to life, veered round and surged heavily downstream – no grayling, this. After running a short distance it slowed; I increased pressure, only for the fish to respond with another uncontrollable surge which carried it several yards further away. A bow of line hung across the water, and well down the swim the float could be seen, cutting slowly across the surface as the confused fish worked ponderously against the current. Very gently, I increased pressure, in the hope of catching a glimpse of whatever I'd hooked; suddenly the water rocked, and the drum of the centrepin began to spin under light finger pressure as several more yards of line vanished.

As yet I had failed to make any impression on the fish, and as it was now quite a distance downstream, I decided to follow, trying to retain a tight line as I stumbled through the thick bankside grasses. On a couple of occasions I caught fleeting glimpses of the fish when it moved into the margins beneath the wilting rushes on the far side, but I never saw enough to enable me to identify it, just a shadow in the murky water before it bow-waved away again. After covering some 40 yards my progress was impeded by a large sallow bush, and some distance below this the fish became firmly snagged. This was an opportunity to leave the rod on the bank while I rushed upstream to collect the landing net, which had been left behind in the excitement.

Upon returning, I picked up the rod and forced past the bush, stooping beneath the low hanging branches, silt churning as I struggled to keep a foothold in the shallow water. Once clear, I walked down to where the fish had buried in a clump of streamer weed, and I pulled from downstream. There was a sudden movement, again I momentarily glimpsed a dark form, and then I had to yield line as the fish forged irresistibly back upstream. At first I decided to bide my time and wait below the bush, for now I had the current on my side. The current, however, seemed to be of little consequence to whatever I'd hooked, for it just ploughed stubbornly onwards, until the drum of the centrepin suddenly stopped revolving. The reel had been loaded with about 40 yards of line, and the fish had taken it all. There was no option but to move upstream, so I grabbed the landing net and pushed past the sallow again. Having done so, I found that the line had become entwined in a sunken branch on the far side of the beck, and it seemed that the fish had run into a snag further upstream, for all movement had ceased. Try as I might, I couldn't free the line from the branch without risking a break, so I laid the rod on the bank and headed off upstream at a brisk trot, in order to find Tony and ask for some assistance.

I found him perhaps a quarter of a mile up the bank; somewhat breathless, I explained the situation, whereupon Tony picked up his landing net and crossed the beck by means of a dilapidated wooden footbridge, while I rushed back downstream. A few minutes later, Tony arrived opposite where I was waiting with rod in hand, and after slithering down the bank, he began to prod around with his landing net. Eventually a slimy, weed-festooned branch was pulled from the water's edge, and after a little careful finger work, Tony announced that the line was free. I wound down, and walked upstream to a point where the tackle was very firmly snagged in mid-stream. The float was now above the water's surface, so I knew that the fish, if still hooked, was not far away. Again Tony stumbled down the bank, and at full stretch, began to poke around with the pole of his landing net. Suddenly the line fell slack, the tackle still intact but the fish gone.

Returning to my tackle, I poured a cup of coffee and sat down to drink it while I recovered composure. Tony headed back up to the bridge, and at length arrived where I was sitting. We discussed the lost fish and agreed that the most likely culprit was a pike, although we'll never know for sure.

Before long I picked up the rod again, and decided to run the float past the raft a few more times. I felt that there might still be fish in the swim which were willing to feed, since all the disturbance had taken place well downstream. By now it was late afternoon and dusk was less than an hour away, although for the time being hazy winter sunshine was illuminating the surroundings. Tony wandered downstream, while I approached the swim and commenced by dropping a handful of loose maggots into the current.

I ran the float through several times before the yellow tip dipped, a yard or two below the raft, and a dace of perhaps a couple of ounces came kicking and splashing across the surface.

Another one followed, then, as the float again brushed past the trailing weed, it stabbed into the flow once more. Tightening, I realised at once that I had a grayling, but there was a heaviness about the struggle which I had never encountered in a grayling before. For a while the fish stayed deep, line cutting swathes in the current, then it turned and forged downstream with several short surges, until it arrived in shallower water at the tail of the pool. I followed, hanging on as the grayling plunged and kited in the flow. Sometimes I caught a fleeting glimpse of a dark back and a large dorsal fin in the tinted water, at other times I saw the pale gleam of a flank. Tony was on hand with the landing net as the fish worked up the margins, furrowing the surface; in a trice he had it engulfed in the meshes.

We carried it up the bank and laid the net among the thick grasses before removing the hook. Dark, lightly flecked, it was a grayling larger than either of us had seen before. We agreed that it might make 2lb, though in truth I expected it to fall an ounce or two short of that figure. Lifting the scales, I watched the needle flicker to a halt at 2lb 7oz; Tony's expression was one of disbelief, and I too had my doubts that the reading was true, so I suggested that we re-weigh the fish on Tony's scales. His verdict was just ¼oz lighter.

I was still in something of a trance when we met at dusk to begin the long walk back through the fields. In a handful of February days I had experienced just about every emotion that angling can provide – all from a tiny, insignificant-looking beck.

8   The Cross Lane Ponds

Three different pools make up the Cross Lane Ponds; here I shall concern myself mainly with the largest, which is roughly square shaped, and rather less than 2 acres in extent. The water is clear and very shallow, with few areas which exceed 4 feet in depth. A thick, soft mantle of blanket weed almost entirely covers the bottom during the summer months, and tactics must be adapted in order to prevent baits from becoming lost among it. There are also some localised beds of milfoil, which grow to the surface in a soft tangle and seem to form a great attraction to the resident coots. Rushes encroach the margins in places, notably along the north bank, which is rather overgrown, overhung by sallows and towering crack-willows, and receives little attention from anglers. On the opposite side of the pool is an old brick farmhouse which overlooks the fishery; there are some well used pitches at the bottom of the garden, but personally I prefer the west bank, which is opposite a busy main road which runs past the pond, and away from the accompanying noise and dust.

The west bank is the location of a narrow clay partition, supported in places by wooden planks and stakes and barely wide enough to enable two men to pass, which separates the two smaller ponds. One of these ponds is cloaked by a mantle of duckweed during the summer months; if the countless tiny leaves are parted, it can be seen that the water beneath is crystal clear, and the bed of the pool is pale, almost bleached in appearance. This is because the duckweed effectively forms a curtain which blocks sunlight, prohibiting the growth of other aquatic plants, and of plankton which would tinge the water. Fish can move in and out of the pond by means of a channel which connects with the large pool.

The third, and smallest pool is completely separate from the other two, and differs in that the water is heavily coloured. Tiny, rush-fringed and overhung by hawthorns, it holds some surprises despite the fact that the depth averages less than 2 feet. I recall catching eight tench there on a still August morning; the largest weighed 3lb 2oz and each, upon feeling the hook, struggled with tenacious power, bow-waving through the shallow water and setting the tiny pond rocking. It is interesting that due to the coloured water, the fish in this pool are very pale in hue compared to those in the two larger pools.

The ponds contain a diversity of fish life. There are roach aplenty, sleek, dark specimens of very pronounced colouration, bronze-tinged flanks and fins of deep scarlet. A handful of carp, and some crucians, are restricted to the two larger pools. There are also some fair bream, and of course the inevitable small perch, jack pike and eels. It was the tench which initially fired my enthusiasm, however; I saw a 3-pounder landed on my first visit, and thereafter I returned several times in a fruitless attempt to catch one. Then, on a warm August morning, I managed to tempt my first tench from the fishery in unlikely circumstances.

I chose to fish the large pool from the partition, float-fishing a maggot on fine tackle in the hope of picking up small roach or skimmers for use as livebaits for pike. Plumbing revealed a depth of 3 feet, so I set the tiny porcupine quill accordingly and began

Result of a morning's fishing on the Cross Lane Ponds – three bream and a solitary crucian carp

fishing. Before long there came a dip of the float, and a roach came kicking and splashing into the margins. Soon after catching it, I became aware of a disturbance in a corner of the duckweed-covered pond.

I pushed through hawthorns to reach the area, where two or three substantial fish were active beneath the duckweed, backs sometimes humping through the tiny leaves. It seemed that I had stumbled upon some of the pool's rare carp, and this was confirmed when I saw, fleetingly, a large blue-grey shape, through a parting in the duckweed.

Making haste back to my tackle, I rigged up a through-action rod, threading 8lb line through the eyes and attaching a number 6 hook direct. Then I crept back through the hawthorns, rod in one hand and landing net in the other, to lower a floating crust amongst the duckweed. A take seemed inevitable, but it wasn't to be; the crust was ignored, despite the fact that dark nebs sometimes pushed through the leaves, mere inches away from the bait. In the end, the carp were driven away by my frustrated attempts to catch them. Since that day I have often watched for movements amongst the duckweed which might betray the whereabouts of a carp, but I have never seen another one in the pool; while they might move undetected beneath the mantle of tiny leaves, it is my belief that they prefer to occupy the large pond.

Returning to the partition, I mashed a slice of bread and lobbed it in, so that it flaked and clouded through the water, to settle upon the blanket weed. This, I hoped, might attract a few bait-sized skimmer bream into the swim. Before long, the tiny quill dipped and sank slowly away. It took a few seconds, after setting the hook, before I realised that I was connected to something more substantial than a skimmer. It gave a deep, powerful struggle, thrusting forcefully and repeatedly down into the Canadian pondweed which grew thickly in the margins. There was a heavy billow beneath the rod end, before a dark tench broke the surface in an oily swirl. It was netted without difficulty, and weighed 2lb 11oz.

After a period of retention in a keepnet, the fish was found to be covered in blood red blotches; these were not cuts or sores, but appeared to be patches of pigment in the skin. Another angler once spoke to me about a similar occurrence with tench caught from a different pond. I suspect that this is a nervous reaction, similar to the two-tone colouration which is sometimes evident in individuals of certain species.

Following this breakthrough, I caught tench on most of my summer visits to the Cross Lane Ponds. On one memorable June day I took twenty of them, probably the heaviest catch of fish I have ever made. They were not retained in a keepnet, but were returned as they were caught. I weighed only the six largest, each of which exceeded 3lb. The average size of the fish was about 2½lb, and I estimate that the total catch would have weighed in the region of 50lb. While the catch gave me great pleasure, I don't enjoy taking large bags of easy fish on a regular basis, and I would soon have tired of the Cross Lane Ponds tench had they always been so simple to tempt.

One species which constantly eluded me during my early years on the ponds was the carp. On occasions I saw them in the large pool, thick-shouldered, slate-grey fish, browsing among the marginal weeds, but it was apparent that they were few in number. They were a challenge, and my desire to catch one gradually increased. I had been close on one occasion, when an immensely powerful specimen took a breadflake bait intended for tench. In the snag-free confines of the pool I thought I had a chance of landing it, until it found sanctuary in a patch of fibrous weed out in the middle. On another occasion I foulhooked a mirror of 12lb 6oz, a beautiful fish of most unusual colouration, back and flanks almost black, giving way to an amber belly.

For some anglers, carp fishing is a lifelong obsession; for me it was a phase, the foundations of which were laid when I had a taste of success during my youth, and which reached a climax during the early 1980s. For two summers I fished for carp exclusively and thought I had found the ultimate in coarse angling, but gradually, at first almost sub-consciously, I began to drift back to general fishing. The 'uncatchable' myth surrounding carp had gone; more and more I saw them as just another fish, no more or less worthy of attention than the species which I had neglected. However, there remained one unfulfilled carp-angling ambition; a fairly hooked fish from the Cross Lane Ponds.

There came a heatwave summer which provided a unique opportunity to achieve this ambition. Oppressive, humid days of blazing sunshine resulted in the carp spending considerable periods of time on the surface, and through careful observation I learnt more about them in the space of a few weeks than I had previously done during several seasons. I came to recognise just five fish; there may have been others, but I am inclined to think not. They appeared to spend most of their time in a little fished corner of the pool, best approached from the overgrown bank, where access was difficult due to the heavily reeded margins.

On a late June day I had the afternoon off work, and I made my first visit of the season to the pond. It was among the earliest of the sweltering days which seemed to recur monotonously throughout that summer, plainly a good opportunity to carry out a little fish spotting.

Walking around the pool on that day was a revelation, with fish of all species, torpid in the heat, clearly visible in the sun-illuminated water. Roach were everywhere, grey shapes clustered in shoals over the dense carpet of blanket weed. There were plenty of nice samples in the ½–1lb range in evidence, but they showed no inclination to feed, and indeed seemed to be disturbed by the loose maggots which I dropped among them. Jack pike hung ominously in the margins; one larger than average fish, of about 8lb, was slinking slowly along the bottom, causing obvious agitation among the milling roach in the vicinity. I saw no sign of bream, and only once did I spot a tench as it burrowed purposefully into the weed, perhaps to seek refuge from the intense sunlight. All the aforementioned fish were of secondary interest, however; I had already spotted what I was looking for, in a thick, soft bed of milfoil beyond congested marginal reeds, in the favoured corner of the pool. Here, a broad-backed mirror carp hung in the sun's warmth, motionless save for a gentle stirring of the pectorals and the rhythmic movement of the gills. It was the largest of the five carp which I subsequently came to recognise, a fish which I am reliably informed had been caught at 19lb, and which looked every ounce of that weight.

I retreated some distance from the water's edge to tackle up, loading a favourite, through-action glass rod of 10 feet in length with 8lb line, which was tied direct to a number 6 hook. Bait was floating crust. I crept back to the reeds and peeped over; the carp was still there. The crust was lobbed a few feet beyond the fish, and then gently drawn back towards it. Long before the bait reached the desired position, however, the carp became suspicious, turned, and disappeared into the soft fronds of milfoil.

145

I waited, watching carefully, looking for a movement in the water or a bulging in the weed to give away the position of the fish. In the hot weather, I didn't expect it to move far, and I felt sure that it would soon be basking again. Numerous rafts of floating algae were present in the corner of the pool, and before long I saw one of them hump and lift a little. I watched like a hawk, but it wasn't the big mirror which eventually moved into view, but a small common of about 5lb. It was equally unresponsive to my efforts.

It became apparent that several carp were moving in the milfoil bed, and that they were very wary of floating crust. After some time spent watching the fish shuffle positions amongst the weed, it became clear that a different bait was needed.

In the car boot was a tin of worms, scratched up from the dry earth a few days previously. A long shot, but they had to be worth a try. I injected one with air to make it float, and returned to my position behind the reeds. The response of the carp was again unfavourable when they encountered the worm in normal circumstances; every so often, however, a fish would begin nosing in a raft of algae, and it seemed that this might present the chance I was looking for. What could be more natural to a carp in such circumstances than a fat worm, for all the world resembling a leech or a larva of some description which was browsing on the algae?

From then on, I resisted the temptation to offer a bait to the carp, except when they were nosing in the algae. Much of the time was spent simply watching and waiting for a fish to move beneath a raft. Even when one did, there were problems, for at such times the carp's vision was completely obscured, so that the bait would remain unnoticed unless positioned directly in front of the fish's mouth. Often, while trying to manoeuvre the bait, the hook would become stuck in the algae; then I had no option but to wait for the carp to move away, for a substantial movement of the raft would probably have scared the fish.

After missing a possible take from the small common, I saw a nice mirror – possibly the one I had foulhooked a couple of years previously – move beneath a raft on the far side of the milfoil bed. A gem of a cast dropped the worm onto the algae, and a little careful twitching drew it to the spot where I could see a dark neb pushing through the scum. The worm became lost to sight, but I

146

THE CROSS LANE PONDS

noticed that the neb appeared to be protruding a little further, and there was an audible sucking noise. I watched the line; it seemed like an eternity before it suddenly twitched, and began to snake across the surface. I struck, and there was a heavy swirl which left the pool rocking, but the hook came back bare and tangled in the bankside foliage.

By now the afternoon was well advanced, and the shadows of the surrounding trees were beginning to finger across the milfoil bed. I found myself regretting the missed chance, for now there was little evidence of carp, although I kept watching in the hope that another one would put in an appearance. Twenty minutes passed before, most unexpectedly, I spotted a fish on the move, very close to the reeds. It made a sudden and abrupt turn, as if it had seen me, and thrust away through the milfoil fronds, but then it doubled back and began to work slowly towards the rushes on my right. Eventually it poked its nose into a raft of algae, just a little beyond the stalks. Creeping closer, I found myself near enough to lower the worm directly onto the raft. Not for the first time that day, the hook became stuck in the algae, but I managed to free it, without disturbing the fish, and I soon had the worm positioned perfectly.

Although I could see only the carp's snout, it was possible to sense the sudden excitement at the moment the fish detected the bait; the gentle stirrings of the algae came to an abrupt halt, and there was a tense pause before the next move took place. The mouth pushed upwards, but slightly to the side of the bait, and the watery suckings were in vain. After backing off for a moment, the fish pushed forward again, and this time located and engulfed the worm.

As the hook sank home the carp erupted from the water, crashing back amid spray and flying algae, before furrowing deep into the milfoil bed. It didn't get far with both the rod and soft masses of weed working against it, however, and soon came wallowing back towards the reeds. I paddled among the stalks so that I could reach a little further with the net. The carp saw me coming and once again thrust away, only to be thwarted once more after moving a few yards. Oozy, black mud stirred beneath my wellington boots, and the aroma of water mint filled the air as I reached forward with the net again. No mistake this time, and the fish was hoisted ashore amid dripping masses of weed.

It was a fine looking carp, pink flanks and a dark, blue-tinted back. It weighed 9¼lb, the smallest of the four mirrors which I came to identify in the pond. I spent the remainder of the evening fishing elsewhere in the pool, pulling out several dark, chunky tench, which fought like dogs and provided an enjoyable conclusion to a good day.

About a month later I was at the pond again, this time with Pete Connor for a tench fishing session. We made a dawn start and soon had fish on the go; lazy streams of bubbles burst on the surface and hung in the scum over our baited swims. It wasn't long before the floats were on the move, and taut lines were zig-zagging through the oily-calm surface in the wake of tenacious fighters.

The author's first carp from the Cross Lane Ponds – a 9¼lb mirror

Although the weather was warm, the sky remained overcast, which undoubtedly contributed towards the fact that we continued to get occasional bites throughout the morning. Our plan was to pack up at lunchtime, enjoy a pub meal and a pint and then return home to catch up on a little lost sleep.

Lunchtime was drawing close when far across the pond, close to the road bank, there was a heavy splash. I watched carefully, and before the ripples had subsided, a great, shuddering brute of a carp hurled itself upwards again. Grabbing my polarising sunglasses, I rushed round to see if any fish could be seen. At least two carp were nosing amongst a small bed of milfoil, not far from the bank. I returned to my tackle, and set up a freeline rig. Then I rooted about in my basket for a tin of Bacon Grill, before I picked up the landing net and headed back round the pool. Before I reached the weedbed, however, I stopped dead in my tracks; browsing over the soft blanket weed, in water barely deep enough to cover its back, was a sizeable carp. It was a long, lean fish which I had not noticed on my previous visits to the pool that season, although I saw it again on several occasions later in the summer. I estimated it to weigh about 16lb, which, I reckoned, made it the second largest carp in the fishery.

I baited with a chunk of Bacon Grill and flicked it out, dropping it delicately onto the surface, just a few feet away from the carp. The meat settled upon the weed, clearly visible, and I waited. It was a matter of minutes before the fish stumbled into the bait and sucked it up without hesitation. My strike pulled the bare hook clean out of its mouth. The fish departed with a heavy swirl, bow-waving out into the pool, and I sunk to my knees in despair.

A few yards further along the bank, I drew close to the weedbed where I had first spotted carp that morning. At least one was still in evidence, so I cast towards it, but thereafter I saw nothing more; perhaps the fish became aware that something was amiss, and departed from the area. For a further twenty uneventful minutes I fished on, watching carefully for any movement which might betray the whereabouts of a carp. Then I saw it, a slate-grey form moving slowly beyond a narrow border of milfoil, tight against the marginal rushes. For a few minutes I lost sight of the fish in the weed, and I waited patiently for it to re-appear. Eventually it emerged and slid a little further out into the pool, where it began browsing over the soft blanket weed; it was without a doubt the same long, lean mirror which I had missed on the strike a little earlier. Out went my bait, delicately, and well in front of the carp. Slowly, the fish worked along the bottom, gradually moving closer to the Bacon Grill but still, as yet, unaware of its presence. The carp then buried its head deep into the blanket weed, and I took advantage of the opportunity to draw the bait to within a foot or so of where it was rooting and digging. A full minute passed before it lifted its head, spotted the bait and immediately sucked it in.

No mistake this time, and I felt the rod bounce in my hands as the hook sank home. Once again the big mirror bow-waved off the shallows, moving out into the pool with a series of short, irresistible lunges until a great bow of line hung across the water. I realised that the carp was getting perilously close to a weedbed out in the centre of the pool, so I swung the rod sideways and leaned in heavily. The efforts of the fish became intensified, and there were several swirls close to the outermost growth, before it turned and began to kite diagonally to the left. Now it headed directly towards the small bed of milfoil in which carp had been moving earlier in the day. I pumped hard, maintaining heavy pressure, and managed to steer the fish clear with only a few feet to spare. Then it blundered into the soft marginal weed to my left, in which it became cocooned and motionless. I moved closer, then Pete took the net and dug into the weed. At first we weren't sure exactly where the fish was, but as Pete lifted, the weed slid apart to reveal a broad tail. A little more prodding and pushing, and we knew that the carp was trapped somewhere amongst the great bundle of weed in the net. We pulled the stuff away in dripping, green handfuls, until the fish lay exposed, a fine specimen of 15lb 13oz. My only complaint was that due to this little escapade, we didn't arrive at the pub in time for lunch!

With a fortnight's holiday due in August, I decided to spend some more time at the pool, in the hope of contacting the largest of the five fish. I had spotted it on several occasions, and each time I had been impressed by its size: the width of its back was such that I felt it might now weigh in excess of 20lb.

On the first day of the vacation, I arrived at the pool soon after dawn, and set up stall in the corner swim. It was a warm, still morning, and a few wisps of mist were drifting across the surface; another hot day was in the offing. I had decided to float-fish, using a loaded dart so that split shot were unnecessary. Thus the bait, a cube of Bacon Grill, was free to sink under its own weight and settle upon the blanket weed. After casting beyond the milfoil bed, I placed the rod in extended rests which served to hold it above the rushes, which were taller and denser than they had been earlier in the season.

There was some surface activity well out in the pool in the form of occasional heavy swirls and bow-waves, but because I couldn't be sure that carp were responsible, I refrained from casting to these fish. It was 8am before I saw definite evidence that carp were around; by then, the sun's warmth was beginning to penetrate, and this encouraged a couple of fish to move into the milfoil bed, their dark, glistening backs humping through the surface. Before long they moved on, and a little later I distinguished two large, pale shapes, drifting slowly beneath the surface reflections, heading gradually towards the bait. As they milled beneath the float, the black tip gave two sharp dips and then vanished, the line tightening behind it. I struck at thin air, and two violent swirls marked the departure of the fish.

After fumbling another cube of Bacon Grill onto the hook, I re-cast. This time the bait settled upon the blanket weed in such a position that I was able to see it, for the water is very shallow in this area; it is only because of glare that sub-surface goings-on often pass unobserved. It wasn't long before I noticed another pale shape moving towards the bait from the open pool. This time I saw the small cube of meat disappear between pouting lips, and simultaneously the slender black tip of the float slipped under. A split second later, however, the float re-surfaced, and a bow-wave headed towards the centre of the pool.

At 9am a light breeze sprang up, barely enough to ruffle the surface, but thereafter the carp showed only fleetingly in the swim. I was aware, though, of occasional activity beyond an exposed willow root to my right, which formed a small promontory, rimmed by rushes. Moving through the undergrowth to investigate, I found the area to be quite impossible to fish, except by casting blindly over the rushes. Since the chance of tempting a carp from elsewhere in the pool seemed to have gone, I decided to clear a channel through the stalks. I knew that this action would probably spook the fish, but I figured that it would make them approachable if they occupied the same area during future sessions. Returning to the car, I exchanged my wellington boots for thigh waders, and I was soon uprooting rushes from the soft, black mud at the bottom of the pool. The growth extended for perhaps 10 feet from the bank, and I aimed to make a channel of about a foot wide. This task took longer than might be expected, for the stalks were tightly clustered. Eventually I reached the outermost growth, the combined depth of water and silt resulting in the tops of my waders sinking to a position perilously close to the surface level. As I uprooted the last of the rushes, I saw to my astonishment that two carp were still basking amid sparse milfoil mere feet from where I stood. One of them was the large fish.

Very slowly, I turned and moved stealthily towards the bank. Once there, I made hasty adjustments to the tackle, removing the float before impaling a fat lobworm on the hook and injecting it with air to make it float. Lying the landing net on the rushes to the side of the newly created channel, I stepped back into the water and proceeded carefully to the edge of the growth. By now, however, the carp were in a highly agitated state, and before long they moved away, having shown no interest in the bait. During the remainder of the summer I didn't have cause to use the channel, for the fish didn't show in the area again.

I made an early start on the pool the following morning, and had two probable takes on Bacon Grill before a breeze sprang up at breakfast time, and thereafter activity diminished. In both cases the float disappeared suddenly and a bow-wave surged away from the area, but the line remained limp. Both times I struck at nothing, the baits apparently having been ejected. It seemed that something was spooking the carp at the moment they took the bait. Could it be the sudden movement of the float above their heads, I wondered? This theory is supported by the fact that the 15lb 13oz fish had confidently accepted a freelined cube of Bacon Grill. The float had seemed an ideal method of bite indication in the weed-choked pool, and a suitable alternative would not be easy to find.

On my next visit I didn't arrive until late morning on another hot, sunny day, when just the lightest of breezes ruffled parts of the surface. One or two carp were moving in and out of the milfoil bed; I tried lying a freelined cube of Bacon Grill on top of the weed, and I also tried an air injected lobworm, but to no avail. Fish which emerged amongst the weed were invariably disturbed

Stalking carp in a lily-choked pool

by my attempts to position a bait nearby, no matter how delicately the operation was performed. The carp were intent on basking rather than feeding, although had I been able to forsee the area in which a fish would surface, and position a bait beforehand, I think it quite likely that a take would have followed. As things were, I was chasing shadows, and it soon became apparent that it was a futile exercise.

As a last resort, I scattered a few Munchies (a small biscuit-type cat food) over the milfoil and in the open water beyond. The response was quite startling. From far out in the pool I saw a dark back cutting a furrow through the surface as a carp moved purposefully towards the floating baits. Before long, three fish were cruising around in the open water, lifting their heads occasionally to sip down a Munchie.

Taken straight from the packet, Munchies are too hard to impale on a hook, so I dropped a few into the margins among the rushes and left them to soak for a few minutes. Meanwhile, I tried to keep the carp interested by catapulting more loose offerings into the swim. Unfortunately, the fish lost interest and drifted away before I had a chance to present a hookbait. Strangely enough, though I tried Munchies on several occasions later in the summer, the carp never again responded.

Another early morning visit to the pool, on a late August day, was to teach me what contrary creatures carp can be. I arrived with the intention of fishing for tench and bream, and accordingly I selected a popular and productive swim on the west bank. Conditions were perfect: warm, still and rather overcast. As I tackled up, there came a sizeable swirl, a short way out in the pool, followed by the distinct, humped back of a carp lifting through the surface. Further observation revealed that several fish were on the move, occasionally pausing to suck at floating debris. While my experiences suggested that floating crust was a completely 'blown' bait, I had nothing else to offer, so I dunked a couple of pieces to add weight and catapulted them into the area in which the fish were showing. To my surprise, it wasn't long before both were sucked down confidently.

Setting up a rig to fish an anchored crust, I baited the hook, cast out and then carefully took up all the slack, until another turn of the reel handle would have submerged the bait. Takes to anchored floaters are often difficult to hit, and while I can offer no explanation based on the physics of the subject, I have found that eliminating slack line increases the percentage of successful strikes. Not so on this occasion, however, for I had four apparently confident takes, and struck at thin air each time. There were several other rather nervous swirls at the crusts, before in mid-morning all carp activity ceased.

In early September the weather finally broke, and on a cool day of blustery wind and driving rain I spent a few hours fishing the small pool in the company of Pete Connor. We struggled to tempt a few small roach and skimmers, along with a solitary, slightly larger bream of a little over the pound. With the passing of the hot summer, the chances of catching another carp seemed to have diminished, and so my quest for the big mirror was postponed until the following season. Little did I know that that wild September day was to be the last I would ever spend fishing for coarse fish on the Cross Lane Ponds.

I had spoken to the lady farmer who owns the fishery on several occasions, and it was apparent that she was dissatisfied with the way the association, to which the fishing was leased, had allowed the banks to become overgrown and unkempt in appearance.

This, combined with the fact that the association paid only a pittance of a rent, resulted in the farmer deciding to terminate the lease when it expired at the end of the year. However, I was informed that the fishing would be available on a day ticket, after a little clearance of the banks had taken place.

Early the following year, I read a few lines in the angling column of a local newspaper, which announced the opening of a new trout fishery. Fearing the worst, I drove to the ponds at the first opportunity, on a cold, blustery April morning. Pulling the car onto the verge, I looked out at a fishery which I barely recognised. A bright, newly painted notice had been erected at the entrance. Many of the trees and bushes had been trimmed or chopped down, and an ugly fisherman's hut stood starkly beside the small pool. Neat gravel paths twisted along the banks, and wooden fishing platforms had been built in various positions, including one in the reedy corner where I had stalked carp less than a year previously.

A lone angler was fishing from one of the farm garden pitches, not far from where I sat. Following a series of false casts, he dropped a lure into the leaden, wind-rippled pool, and began to work it back towards the bank in a series of slow draws. A flurry of snowflakes began to flutter down from heavy, grey skies. Huddled against the cold, the angler cast again; before long his line straightened, and a bright silver rainbow cartwheeled out of the water.

It was all very different to the Cross Lane Ponds of which I had grown so fond. I don't think I could bring myself to fish there at present, even though I have been known to dabble with a fly rod on occasions. As for the coarse fish, some reports suggest that they were transferred elsewhere by the water authority, but a reliable acquaintance tells me that he has seen carp in the large pool since the fishery opened for trout angling. So perhaps the big mirror still basks amid the milfoil on sultry summer days, untouchable now, and further from my grasp than ever.

Conclusion

Hidden among trees beside a farm building was a small pond, fringed by alders and studded with lilies. I fished it on just a handful of occasions, invariably disturbing a group of domestic geese, which would waddle noisily into the water as I approached. Usually they made for the sanctuary of an island where sycamores and more alders clamoured for the available space, leafy boughs overhanging the surface; this was also a favourite haunt of moorhens when they weren't busy elsewhere in the pool, strutting with jerking gait from lily pad to lily pad.

A pinch of breadflake fished beneath a slim quill invariably drew a response from roach, mint-fresh specimens, sleek and bronze-tinged. Small perch were a menace when worms or maggots were used as bait. Once, the slate-grey form of a carp appeared fleetingly from beneath the marginal lily pads close to where I was fishing.

One summer morning, I promised myself, I would make a dawn start at the pool and attempt to catch a carp, or perhaps one of the tench which were rumoured to be present. Then came news of a chemical spillage at the farm.

There was some confusion as to whether or not the wipe-out had been total, so three years later I returned to the pond to find out. The neglected bankside track had been encroached by a jungle of briers, and the branches of untended trees had almost blocked the path in places. The once prolific lilies had vanished, save for a small cluster close to the place where the carp had shown. Nothing stirred; no creature which dwelt in the pool had survived that fateful day.

The threat of a similar catastrophe haunts every coarse fishing water. Those which have escaped exist only subject to the whims of man and the quirks of nature, while any fishery might suffer because of influential people who feel that change is desirable.

The message is clear: when the opportunity to fish a special water arises, take it. Tomorrow the chance may have gone.

Acknowledgements

My interest in angling began at the tender age of 7, the result of a friendship made at primary school. John Chrispin introduced me to the subtle art of catching bullheads and stone loach, by hand, from beneath overturned rocks in the Crimple Beck. Later we progressed to rod and line fishing for minnows and sticklebacks, and eventually for the wild brown trout which haunted the deep pools.

Since then there have been many friends who have influenced my approach to the sport and who have, directly or indirectly, played a role in the preparation of this book. In particular I would like to thank Alan Thomas, Tim Moulds, Pete Connor, Rob Platais, Jon Wolfe, Dave Martin, Steve Fairbourn, Martin Flowers, Mick Beecroft, Dave Wilkinson, Steve Rhodes, Steve Willis, Dave Jones, Roland Froebel, Simon Linley and last but not least Tony Smith.

Thanks also to Sandy Leventon and Bruce Vaughan of the now defunct magazine, *Coarse Fishing Monthly*, for the encouragement they gave by publishing some of my early articles. Also to Colin Dyson and Bruno Broughton, of *Coarse Angler*, for publishing my current work and for permission to use some photographs which have previously appeared in the magazine. And finally to my brother Mike, who supplied the jacket photograph along with several others.

Index

Accrington, 101
Algae, fishing in, 146–7
Arlesey Bomb, 39

Bacon Grill, for carp, 149, 151, 152;
  for catfish, 97, 99, 101
Bait, *see* Specific types
Bait additives, 112–13
Bait dropper, 86, 90, 92, 93
Barbel, 34, 81–95, *82*, *94*
Barbless hooks, method of securing
  livebaits, 120
Bites, roach, 113; tench, 23–4, 27
Bivvies, 49
Bobbins, 19, 62
Bread, 38–9, 49, 55, 71; crust, 39, 41,
  72, 75; flake, 20, 28, 41, 43, 44, 50,
  144; floating crust, 143, 145–6,
  154; mash, 20, 39, 41, 43, 44, 49,
  67, 75, 143
Bream, 30, 34, 48, 51, 55, 66, 69–71,
  74–80, *79*, 96–7, *142*, 145; as bait,
  99
Briggs Pit, 11–32, *27*
Buckingham, 100, 104
Buckinghamshire, 96
Buzzer, 50

Canals, 10
Carp, *8*, 28, 48, 52–3, 56–61, *60*, 62,
  64, 66–9, 70–6, *75*, 96–8, 104,
  142–55, *148*
Carp, Crucian, 18, *142*
Carp sacks, 46
Caster, 71, 75; for perch, 36; for
  roach, 27–8, 121, 124
Catfish, 96–107, *100*, *103*
Chalk streams, 9; *see also* Oak Beck
Chub, 30, 34, 35, 39–*45*, 81, 85–6,
  89–92, *90*

Claydon Lake, 96–107
Connor, Pete, *114*, 118, 150
Crimple Beck, 33
Cross Lane Ponds, the, 141–55, *153*
Crumb, brown, 49, 67, 71

Dace, 34, 35, 36, 38, 44, 81, 139; as
  bait, 130, 135
Dacron, for catfish, 97; for eels, 120
Deadbaits, for catfish, 97, 99; for eels,
  120
Deep hooking, author's favoured
  procedure, 116–17

Eel, 18, 30, 38–9, 42, 113, 116, *117*,
  118, 120, 123, 142; as bait, 102
Estate lakes, 10; *see also* Claydon Lake

Flavouring, for maggots, 132
Float-paternoster, 120, 121, 124
Floats, 64, 65; balsa, 82, 86; betalight,
  49, 52; canal crystal, 97; dart, 151;
  driftbeater, 68; for carp, 152; for
  tench, 20; goose quill, 20; marker,
  75; pike, 11, 13, 15, 16, 21, 129;
  porcupine quill, 24, 142; sliding,
  108, 110, 121; stick, 36, 39, 42, 44,
  128
Floods, effect on roach, 33–4
Foamed polystyrene, application for
  fishing in weed, 68

Garwood, Pete, *17*
Gravel pits, 7; *see also* Lagoon
Grayling, 34, 35, 81, 127–9, 131–4,
  137, 140; as bait, 130
Groundbait, 25, 52; commercial,
  112–13; for bream, 71, 75; for
  perch, 110; *see also* Bread and
  Crumb

Gudgeon, 35, 104; as bait, 118, 120, 124

Hemp, 49, 71, 75
Hooklengths, for chub, 39; *see also* Dacron
Hooks, 49, 67; for barbel, 82, 84, 86, 93, 95; for carp, 58, 62, 68, 73, 143, 145; for chub, 39, 43, 90; for grayling, 128, 132; for livebait, 97, 110; for perch, 18, 36, 110; for pike, 129; for roach, 44; for tench, 20, 24, 28; *see also* Barbless hooks

Keepnets, 46
Knaresborough, 81

Lagoon, the, 48–80
Landing nets, 116, 120, 131
Line, for barbel, 82, 84, 86; for carp, 53, 58, 62, 67, 73, 143, 145; for chub, 39, 43, 90; for grayling, 132; for livebait, 97, 110; for perch, 18, 36, 110; for pike, 129; for roach, 44; for tench, 20, 22, 24, 28
Line bites, 77–8
Line clip, 50
Linley, Simon, 48–55, *54*, *57*
Livebait, for catfish, 101, 104; for perch, 110, 118, 120, 121; for pike, 11, 15–16, 130, 135, 142

Maggot, 49, 55, 64, 77; for barbel, 82; for chub, 90; for grayling, 128, 132; for livebait, 13, 97, 110, 142; for roach, 35; for rudd, 57, 61; in bait dropper, 92; in groundbait, 75; method of preparing floaters, 67
Monkey climber indicator, 50, 99
Moulds, Tim, *17*
Munchies, 153
Mussel, swan, 101

Nidd, River, 33, 81–95, *87*, 127

Oak Beck, 127–40, *128*, *136*
Optonic, 49, 99
Oxford, 98, 99

Paddy, 12, 20, 28–30, *31*
Perch, 14, 16–19, *17*, 21, 25, 30, 34–8, 77, 108, 110–12, 118–26, *119*, 142
Pike, 11–19, *14*, *17*, 30, 32, 48, 49, 61, 65, 96, 127, 129–31, *133*, 135–6, 142, 145; small jacks, 25–6
Platais, Rob, 81–5, 100–7
Plug, 30

Quarry pools, 10
Quivertip, 38

Reels, centrepin, 37, 42, 128; fixed spool, 86
Rhodes, Steve, 127
Rivers, rain-fed, 9–10; *see also* Nidd and Wharfe rivers
Roach, 14, 24, 27–8, 30, 33–9, 42–7, *45*, 104, 113–15, 123, 125, *126*, 142, 145; as bait, 15, 16, 97, 101, 105, 118, 121
Rods, Avon, 49, 58, 62, 67, 71, 86; carp, 145; match, 49, 68, 128; quivertip, 44
Rudd, 18, 30, 48, 55, *57*, 58, 61–2, 76; as bait, 11, 14
Ruffe, 18, 38, 42

Swallow Pool, 108–26, *109*
Shot, 58; for float fishing, 82, 97, 115; for legering, 38, 44, 62, 64; to suspend bait, 65, 67, 72, 77
Smith, Tony, 108, *136*, 136–40
Snap tackle, 32
Spinner, 123
Sprat, 32, 129
Squid, 101, 105
Stret-pegging, 34, 36
Sweetcorn, 49, 52, 55; for carp, 56, 58, 62, 68, 71; for tench, 64, 71
Swimfeeder, 43, 49, 71, 72

Tench, 14, 19–28, *21*, *29*, 51, 52, 53, 55, 63, 65–6, *70*, 71, 73–4, *75*, 80, 96, 142–5, 148
Trout, brown, 81
Trout, rainbow, 155

159

Weed, fishing in, 65–9
Wharfe, River, 33–47, *35*, 127
Wheat, stewed, 71
Wire traces, for eels, 120; for pike, 18, 129
Woburn Abbey Lakes, 96
Wolfe, Jon, 118, *119*, 123–6

Worm, 38–9; for carp, 146, 152; for livebait, 13; for perch, 19, 110; for pike, 25–6

Yorkshire, 33, 36, 81, 83

Zander, 96, 104, *105*